The
Music Educator
and
Community Music

The
Music Educator
and
Community Music

The Best of MEJ

Michael L. Mark, Editor

MUSIC EDUCATORS NATIONAL CONFERENCE

Book design by Karen M. Fields

Contents

Section 4   Opportunities for Music Educators

Introduction

American communities embrace a wealth of musical opportunities. Choruses, bands, orchestras, ethnic ensembles, instruction in voice, instruments, appreciation, history, theory, and other areas of music are common elements of a thriving musical life outside the schools. This cornucopia of musical offerings comes from senior centers, recreation departments, fraternal orders, school and adult education programs, community colleges, civic associations, religious organizations, YMCAs and YWCAs, and many other agencies. Community music is available to all who wish to participate, and those fortunate enough to live in musically rich communities often have the opportunity to take part in music activities from early childhood through old age.

Is there a logical and compelling relationship between school music and community music? School music takes place in schools, and community music usually involves adults who are no longer in school. Why should the vast majority of American music educators, who have been trained to teach music to children in school settings, be concerned about musical activities that take place outside the school? Like so many other professional judgments, the answer to this question must come from each individual music educator. The Music Educators National Conference (MENC) has published this compilation of articles from the *Music Educators Journal* (as well as one from its predecessor, the *Music Supervisors Journal*) to provide a reference for music educators as they explore their relationships to community music.

Before delving into the articles, you might find it helpful to remember that music education in American schools is supported by the community in several ways. One of the most obvious reasons for community support is the desire of the public for its children to be musically educated, at least to the point where they can participate as performers or listeners. Communities across the country support music education through demonstrations of interest and encouragement for student musicians. Communities also support school music by paying for it. Music education is an expensive activity that adds significantly to the cost of education. Yet, for well over a century, communities have demonstrated their willingness to shoulder the cost of music in schools.

The school-community relationship is reciprocal. Many communities are musical because of their excellent school music programs. Community musicians have received wonderful musical benefits from participating in school music, and they express their appreciation by supporting a musical life in the community beyond the high school. These people are often the strongest supporters of school music, and an alliance between them and school music educators can reap huge and rewarding harvests, not only in musical terms but also in maintaining community support.

Many music educators keep the community in mind as they plan their educational activities because they feel the need for their programs to satisfy community needs. Those needs differ from one locale to another, but the strong American tradition of state and local control ensures that schools provide for the educational requirements of their communities as defined by local boards of education. Music educators who remain constantly aware of the relationship between school and community music are in a position to develop rewarding relationships with community music leaders and activities to enrich the lives of all musicians in the community, students and adults alike.

Throughout much of the twentieth century, relations between school music and community music have varied from close cooperation to benign neglect. During an earlier time in American history when there was no school music, community music was the basis of virtually all music education. The singing schools provided music instruction for many Americans in colonial New England, where a common purpose of music education was to prepare adults to participate musically in religious services. Adults fulfilled an important part of their community responsibility by singing well in church. Singing schools, especially as they were brought into the Shenandoah Valley of Virginia and the rural South, were also social gatherings where young people could meet and court, and the tradition offered many people a chance to sing for pleasure.

As the public schools began to replace the singing schools throughout the nineteenth century, they, too, emphasized religious music, although to a lesser extent. Community life was stressed in nineteenth-century school music literature, which included songs intended to sensitize children to the beauty of music and to instill moral values, patriotism, love of family, and respect for the community.

School performing ensembles have always entertained their communities and contributed to community functions. Since the latter part of the nineteenth century, school bands, orchestras, and choruses have participated in community life by presenting concerts and programs both in and away from the school. When nineteenth-century Americans discovered how magnificent music could be when performed by European artists such as Jenni Lind and Ole Bull, and when they heard a new American genre of music as performed by the traveling bands of John Philip Sousa, Patrick Gilmore, Patrick Conway, and others, they wanted to emulate these world-class performances in their own communities. The logical vehicles for this

were the school music organizations, many of which were entirely capable of performing difficult music in a musical manner. There was already a precedent in the school choruses of the latter nineteenth century: many of these groups sang the best available European choral literature.

During the days before television and movies with sound tracks, communities across the country invested their pride, love, and scarce financial resources in school performing ensembles. In many cases, music was the primary source of community pride, often overshadowing sports. To a great extent, the close relationship between school music programs and their communities is what enabled music education to flourish and grow into what it is now.

One should not think, however, that the only music available in communities throughout the country was that of school ensembles. Americans were musical people long before Europeans brought their musical traditions to the New World. Native peoples in North America had rich and varied oral musical traditions, and African and Asian contributions to American music have been remarkable and enduring.

The vibrant American colonial music cultures in New England and Virginia, the various German groups in Pennsylvania and the Shenandoah region, and the Dutch in the Hudson River Valley were complemented by settlers from many countries who contributed their own highly valued native musics and cultures. In the New World, music from "the old country" helped satisfy the need of immigrants to live within their familiar cultures as much as possible. European art music flourished as well. Virtually every community, no matter how small, had a piano teacher. Teachers of voice and instruments, trained to high levels in other countries, settled in communities of all sizes across the United States. Their students eventually formed bands, choruses, and orchestras in both schools and communities. Sometimes these ensembles consisted of both students and adults.

The relationship between school and community was strengthened when early leaders of the Music

Supervisors National Conference (MSNC), later the Music Educators National Conference, decided that the organization would be well served by promoting community singing. Peter Dykema, one of the first presidents of the organization, championed the idea in the *Music Supervisors Journal*, which he edited. The MSNC began to gain national stature as it helped promote the community singing movement. Dykema was chairman of the Community Song Committee, established in 1913. He believed that singing should be a part of community life and that children should know the songs that were sung in the community. An early issue of the *Journal* contained an article by Dykema titled "Community Christmas." Music educators reported successful community sings in several parts of the country, and promotional ideas were presented in a feature Dykema called "For Your Local Papers."

When the United States entered World War I, community sings featuring patriotic songs flourished across the country, further increasing the influence of the MSNC. By 1913, the MSNC Community Music Committee had compiled and released *18 Songs for Community Singing*, which was so well received by the public that in 1917 it was expanded to *55 Songs for Choruses and Community Sings* (published, as was the first book, by C. C. Birchard of Boston), and later to *Twice 55 Community Songs*. *Twice 55* was released just before the United States entered the war, and the book become a pillar of the community singing movement. The Liberty edition was published shortly after American entered the war, and it, too, was enthusiastically accepted by the public. The patriotic rallies that produced huge crowds anxious to support the war effort made other publishers aware of the commercial potential of community singing, and they produced such collections as Hall and McCreary's *Golden Book of Favorite Songs*.

Community sings gave people an opportunity to express their patriotism by singing rousing national songs. They also proclaimed their sense of community by sharing songs that were part of the common American musical heritage. Thanks to the MSNC, the American public knew many of the traditional songs of the nation that were part of the standard fare at giant war-bond rallies. These events raised large amounts of money for the war effort and helped elevate both civilian and military morale. Hamlin Cogswell, supervisor of music in Washington, D.C., reported conducting a "chorus" of thirty-two thousand citizens in a carol sing in front of the Treasury Building in the nation's capital during the week before Christmas in 1917.

Military singing paralleled civilian community sings, and more than thirty thousand soldier song leaders were trained to be military song leaders. During the second year of the war, 1918, thirty-seven thousand soldiers attended gatherings in Y.M.C.A. huts, where mass singing was not only the main attraction but frequently the only one.

Trained song leaders were sent into the war industries, where workers in factories sang at noon and during rest periods. Industrial settings for community singing became routine, and many industries set aside time each week for this healthy activity. Many Americans remember community singing in movie theaters ("follow the bouncing ball") as a regular part of numerous short features along with the cartoons and serials. By 1930, the community singing movement had dissipated somewhat, although community singing remained in workplaces and movies well beyond mid-century.

For the four years during which the Second World War was fought against the Axis powers and Japan, the relationships among communities, schools, and government, including the military, remained strong, and music was again called into service as a morale-booster on the home front.

As more community music activities developed throughout the nation, they frequently paralleled musical experiences offered in schools. This was to be expected, because most of the participants were trained in school music organizations. In addition, most of the music directors were also school music teachers. During the latter part of the nineteenth century and throughout the twentieth century, community choruses, bands, and orchestras have flourished. Americans have continually demonstrated their love for music not only by participating in these groups, but by agreeing to support them with their taxes. Perhaps the most striking example is the Iowa Band Law, which provided funds from state tax revenues to support local community bands. This was an unusual legislative action taken in response to the wishes of voters, who had the highest regard for community bands and did not want to be deprived of them. Band enthusiasts will recognize the title of the law as the name of a march written in its honor by bandmaster and composer Karl King.

Today there is a rich variety of community music opportunities throughout the country. These opportunities continue to complement music opportunities in schools. In the best situations, school and community music leaders work together to maintain a strong community musical life.

There is a question, however, of the proper relationship between school and community music. Many communities offer people the opportunity to participate in the same kinds of ensembles that are available in the schools. This duplication of music activities is most often seen in the entertainment aspect of the music program. Many, perhaps most, community organizations accept students as members. If students can participate in similar music entertainment activities in the community, then school music educators might take advantage of opportunities to give up some of their entertainment activities and concentrate more on the solid musical aspects of their programs.

An example can be found in the drum and bugle corps groups found in communities throughout much of the country. Students in communities with strong drum and bugle corps often must choose whether to participate in the school marching band or a drum and bugle corps, perhaps sponsored by a local American Legion or Veterans of Foreign Wars post. This is an example of duplication of effort that could be avoided if some schools let the community handle an expensive, time-consuming, and primarily entertainment aspect of music performance and redirected the marching band resources to other musical activities.

Such an argument does not denigrate marching bands. Indeed, marching bands provide a healthy and wholesome recreational outlet for hundreds of thousands of students. If, however, a community is willing to sponsor the same activity, there is little reason for the schools to compete.

Another example can be found in the excellent barbershop choruses active throughout the nation. These groups provide wonderful recreational and community-building activities for many people, including students, who want to have fun through music. If high school students are welcome in community barbershop choruses, then the schools might take advantage of the opportunity, not duplicate what already exists, and use their own resources for different musical activities. Of course, not every community offers high-quality musical experiences to large numbers of people. In those that do, though, music educators would do well to consider consolidating their offerings with those of the community so effort and expense can be invested in different musical activities.

Regardless of whether there are competitive aspects between school and community, music educators should be aware of the musical life of the community outside the school. For the sake of their school music programs, they need to know what opportunities are available for their students before and after graduation and how school and community can help each other. The community also offers music educators numerous opportunities to maintain and develop their own music skills. Music educators who participate in or lead community music activities get to know their communities in a way that they could not if they remained in their schools for their entire musical lives.

The articles that follow offer insights into community music that can help music educators understand what resources are available to them outside the schools. I hope that these writings will impel readers to consider that they have opportunities to enrich their communities even more than they do through their professional lives.

Michael L. Mark is dean of the Graduate School at Towson State University, Towson, Maryland.

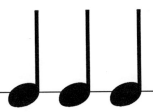

Section

Community Music
in an Earlier Time

This section contains three articles, one by MENC's fourth president, Peter W. Dykema, and two by sociology and music professor Max Kaplan. They offer a look at how things stood with the music education community in 1934 and 1956.

Music in Community Life

by P e t e r W. D y k e m a

Both as regards music and many other social activities, the year 1933 stressed the community idea to an extraordinary extent. The community is asserting itself in new ways as to how its affairs shall be carried on. Negatively, it has insisted on retrenchments in civic business, including in many instances the schools; positively, it has proceeded to build up and support as public enterprises affairs that heretofore have been almost exclusively private. Sometimes these organizations are part of the governmental setup; sometimes wholly private. In a number of cities, such as Washington, [D.C.], Scranton and Wilkes-Barre [in Pennsylvania], and Meriden, Connecticut, well-chosen and widely-directed civic music committees have been formed and have taken an active part in planning the music for the community. There is abundant evidence that this tendency will develop rapidly in the next few years. It is being greatly accentuated by that national government, both through the committees appointed by national agencies and the adaptation of this

procedure by local communities. Despite certain fatalities in municipal music due to the continued depression such as the discontinuance of the Municipal Bureau of Music in Philadelphia, this movement still persists strongly in such cities as Baltimore, where the city continues supporting the Baltimore Symphony Orchestra and the allied symphonic and choral work among colored citizens.

In the past twelve months, unprecedented measures have been undertaken by governmental agencies, working, they believe, in accordance with the inevitable economic trends, to shorten the working week for the great majority of people. Forty-, thirty-five-, thirty-, and even twenty-

---

Peter W. Dykema (1873–1951) was the first editor of the Music Supervisors Journal, *the president of the Music Supervisors National Conference from 1917 to 1919, the author of several books on music and music instruction, and an ardent supporter of community music. Dykema taught at the New York Ethical Culture School, the University of Wisconsin–Madison, and Columbia University in New York. This article originally appeared in the March 1934* Music Supervisors Journal.

This article is taken from the 1933 report of the Committee on Community Music of the Music Teachers' National Association. The report, which is a combination of material prepared by the chairman with the assistance of Kenneth S. Clark, Glenn Tindall, and Augustus D. Zanzig, members of the committee, was given by Mr. Dykema at the convention held in Lincoln, Nebraska, December, 1933, and appears in the M.T.N.A. *Volume of Proceedings,* now in press—a valuable book, by the way.

The article is published not only because of its general interest as a report of developments in the field of community music or "socialized music" as it is referred to by Mr. Dykema—but it also has special significance in view of the plans projected by the Music Supervisors National Conference Committee on Music in Leisure Time, of which Mr. Dykema and Mr. Zanzig are members. The preliminary report of the latter committee will be made at the conference in Chicago, and will be published in the next issue of the journal.   *—The Editors.*

five-hour weeks are now common in the case of great numbers of our working people. The resulting free hours have caused wide discussion of what to do with this leisure time. The appointment by the President of a Leisure Time Committee in New York City, headed by Raymond B. Fosdick, has led to a host of comments. In September a National Education–Recreation Council was formed, at least tentatively, in this city, by representatives of all the well-known social and other agencies whose work has bearing on the leisure time of people. In addition to the Scouts, the Ys, settlements, boys' clubs, adult education associations, the Music Teachers' National Association, Music Supervisors National Conference, and like groups, the Federal Council of Churches and the National Education Association were represented. In a number of cities, there have been formed committees as widely representative of local agencies as this one is of national organizations. The December 1933 issue of the magazine *Recreation* is devoted to this topic and contains most interesting addresses and quotations from articles long and short.

Certain ideas emerge from this discussion that may well be applied to music. *First*, the new leisure time will undoubtedly give great numbers of our people the opportunity for carrying on activities that were difficult if not impossible with the longer working day. *Second*, the essence of leisure is the spirit of doing what one cares or chooses to do rather than what one dislikes or is forced to do. *Third*, there is already considerable suspicion, if not resentment, concerning planned leisure activities. As one of the articles states in connection with the formation of the New York Committee on the Use of Leisure Time, "Leisure is, or should be, whatever the individual cares to make it. May it be pertinent to suggest that what he does is none of the business of Mr. Whalen or his Committee." Another article states that the name of the Committee sounds like a "public welfare satire." *Fourth*, on the other hand, nobody seems to object to there being facilities and materials provided for leisure-time activity, provided these do not press too hard upon the taxpayer. Adequate

playground equipment, libraries with plenty of books, free concerts, free museum, and spectacles of various kinds—all of these are acceptable, providing each individual may decide whether or not he will make use of them and what he will do with them. In other words, it is quite proper to provide excellent water for the horse to drink, but he must decide whether he will drink it.

From these four principles we may deduce certain ideas that need consideration in discussing music in leisure time:

First, there should be more and better musical opportunities for all people. It ought to be possible to have finer concerts to which people will listen more intelligently and appreciatively. There should be many more opportunities for singing and playing by individuals in large and small groups with work of higher quality than we have had heretofore. Creative music in the sense of original compositions should blossom in many unexpected spots. There should be more consideration given to means of starting adults on the study and practice of music. There are thousands of adults who would welcome above every other musical activity the opportunity to learn to play the piano. All of these activities are, however, dependent [on] there being a desire to participate in them. This ideas is of great significance for the teachers of music who have students who are obliged by program or parental influence to study music. This includes most of the school and private teachers of the young. Their teaching must now be conceived more than ever before in terms of developing such a love that the student will wish to continue with it after he is beyond the period of compulsory study.

Eventually, I believe, one valuable measure of the success of all teaching will be the voluntary continuing of it by the student. This would suggest, in other words, that a teacher is successful from this point of view, whose pupils keep on singing or playing years after the lessons have been discontinued.

Second, a deduction may be drawn from this principle when dealing with adults. They must have enough voice in the musical activities contemplated to feel they have in a large measure chosen material and even approach.

Third, there must be less advocating of musical activities in leisure time as a cultural and righteous thing to do, but more as something that increases the joy of living. Music must be so attractive that people will want to have it for its own sake rather because it will make them wiser or more socially prominent. Other effects beyond the joy of the moment will surely follow, as anyone who knows elevating music will testify, but with this new and self-conscious public, that must be something that they themselves will discover after they have voluntarily submitted themselves to the influence of music.

Fourth, we must do all we can to provide better facilities for the production of music. The municipalities must see to it that music demands equipment just as sports do. A concert hall is comparable to a playground in providing opportunities for music. Band and orchestra instruments are as necessary as the swings and other apparatus on the playground. Competent music leaders are more necessary, probably, than directors of sports. The newer music activities will need more adequate music equipment.

Relief Funds and Music

In New York City, there has been established a symphony orchestra of musicians who until its organization had been mainly unemployed. These players are now paid out of funds appropriated through the State Department of Education. The same sort of orchestra and support have been established in Buffalo and perhaps in some other cities in the state. Small instrumental and vocal ensembles and about forty music leaders for settlements, mothers' clubs, and other groups especially needy of recreation leadership are also being paid, through the State Department of Education, for work in New York City.

A large fund was recently appropriated for the Pennsylvania Department of Public Instruction for the development of similar projects in the cities in that state. In Wilkes-Barre, York, Allentown, and Reading, music leaders have been or are about

to be engaged to conduct musical activities in community centers. (This fund is for the whole field of adult education, not for music alone.) The music leaders chosen are from among the unemployed, but, in New York City at least, institutes and other means of further training for these leaders have been provided. The possibilities in all this are [as of December, 1933—the time this paper was written] in very large measure still to be realized. The new federal Civil Works Service is likely to provide funds for the employment of musical as well as other educational and recreational leaders in all the states.

A number of new civic orchestras whose players receive no remuneration have been formed in the past year, notably in Bloomfield, New Jersey, and York, Pennsylvania, in both of which places very commendable concerts have been given to large audiences. The Westchester County, New York, Chamber Music Society, under the auspices of the County Recreation Commission, has one interesting procedure in its program. At intervals of about a month, the various quartets come together at the County Center in White Plains. There they hear an excellent organization, frequently a professional one, play a composition upon which all the groups have been working. Following this, all the groups in a large ensemble repeat the composition under the leadership of the model quartet.

National Music Week

The permanence of the Music Week movement has been attested by the gratifying extent to which the plan was carried out during the week of May 7-13, 1933, despite the fact that conditions made it impossible for the National Music Week Committee to give its usual degree of active guidance to the movement. A lack of funds for the purpose made it necessary for the committee to limit its activities largely to general announcements of the 1933 plans, with special service where this was requested by the local committees. Notwithstanding this lack of propulsion from the national headquarters, the local Music Week continued with a surprising record of accomplishment, despite a similar lack of funds locally.

An example of the beneficial results of the recent Music Week is that in Oregon, where the success of the statewide celebration has resulted in a joint campaign for music festivals throughout the state on the part of the Oregon Federation of Music Clubs and the State Board of Education. Last May's Music Week in Oregon resulted in countywide festivals and contests among the schools of eleven counties. The general observance of Music Week was recorded by two hundred cities or towns in thirty-four counties. In one county the children came a distance of more than one hundred miles to take part in the festival. The success of the 1933 Music Week in advancing music in the various communities as a wholesome form of recreation has resulted in the choice of the following slogan for the 1934 observance: "A More Fruitful Use of Leisure Through Music."

Male Chorus Progress

Not even the acute results of the depression prevented a continuance of the stimulus to "more and better glee clubs" provided by the Associated Glee Clubs of America. That federation of the male choruses of the country staged a number of important massed concerts during this period, including the following: a program by 350 singers from eight clubs of the Hudson Valley at Newburg, New York; the sixth annual state "sing" in Grand Rapids by 418 singers of the Michigan Male Chorus Association, in conjunction with the North Central Music Supervisors Conference; the annual contest and concert of the New England Federation, with 700 men in the massed chorus; the tenth festival of the American Union of Swedish Singers, with a chorus of 800, at Chicago; a program of the New England Federation before the Rotary International convention in Boston, and the first get-together of the Allied Male Choruses of eastern Pennsylvania at Stroudsburg.

General financial and political conditions made impossible the realization of plans for the Intercollegiate Musical Council for an intercollegiate and international student festival at Chicago during A Century of Progress. However, the regular contest activities of the American clubs were carried on during the season, culminating in the national competition at St. Louis in which the winner was the glee club of Pomona College in California, the members of which had traveled three days and two nights in a day coach in order to be present. This final contest was prefaced by ten sectional meets in which 150 colleges participated, with a total of approximately 4,500 singers. At the present moment, the plans for a national contest for 1934 are in abeyance, but the sectional meets will continue as usual.

A feeder for this college movement and a stimulus to better singing in the boys' preparatory schools is the present system of joint festivals by their glee clubs, as instanced particularly by the successful festivals of the New England schools. The policy is to encourage these festivals among the schools if they prove to be more efficacious than the contest movement, which was the initial impetus to better singing among the private schools for boys.

Women's Chorus Activities

Leaders in the development of a similar movement among women's groups are the National Congress of Parents and Teachers, with its stimulus toward the formation of Mother-Singers Choruses among the local P.T.A. groups; and the General Federation of Women's Clubs, with its campaign not only for better informal singing at club meetings but for the development of club chorals. The Federation also stimulated club singing by state choral contests.

An example of a kindred activity among colored groups, but covering mixed choruses, is the annual church choir contest conducted by the Manual Training School at Bordentown, New Jersey. A similar accomplishment of this sort is the third annual choral contest by church choirs and high school choruses under the auspices of the Fiske University Music School in Nashville, Tennessee.

Adult Music Training

State organizations are now giving attention to the matter of providing musical training for adults, for their own enjoyment or in connection with emergency relief work. For instance, the State Extension Department of Massachusetts has arranged for an adult class, under the direction of Dr. Sigmund Spaeth, on the subject of "The Art of Enjoying Music." Relief funds are being used by the New York State Committee for the purpose of training unemployed musicians in the directing of group piano classes, which are in part to be composed of adults. In Montana, the plan is to use unemployed music teachers in nursery schools for children whose mothers are working under re-employment plans. It is also planned in that state to have musical activity during the noon hour at sewing rooms and other places where people are working on relief projects.

Although financial conditions have cut down the amounts of money available for carrying on musical activities among industrial and commercial employees, the music-in-industry movement still continues, largely upon the initiative of the employees themselves and their active interest in music projects already started.

Christmas Caroling

Christmas caroling by groups of "waits" continued in many towns, together with ambitious allied programs in some cities. An example of the latter was the sixteenth Christmas festival at Flint, Michigan, which was a composite affair with the general title of "A Yuletide Festival of Song." In Louisville, there was a central carol program around a municipal tree that was broadcast to the citizens in their homes.

A statewide promotion of Christmas music activities for 1933 was planned by the California Federation of Women's Clubs under the auspices of its music committee.

Helping Agencies

The National Bureau for the Advancement of Music, 45 West 45th Street, New York City, and the Music Department of the National Recreation Association, 315 Fourth Avenue, New York City, continue to be the two agencies that, through correspondence, offer aid to all inquirers. In addition to this, the Recreation Association offers the service of an organizer[1] on a cost basis.

A recent announcement states that the Association is prepared to aid in the planning and administration of the various kinds of musical activities in communities, recreation centers, playgrounds, schools, homes, churches, clubs, and wherever else people may sing, play, or listen for the love of it. This aid can be given through demonstrations, institutes, conferences, and lectures or addresses, and also through surveys of the musical activities and resources already existing in the community.

Note

1. Mr. A. D. Zanzig, who is in charge of this work, is chairman of the Music Supervisors National Conference Committee on School Music in Community Life.

In part 1 of this two-part series of articles, Max Kaplan discusses the nature of change in American society and how it affects community values. He describes two opposing positions on the role of the music educator in the musical life of the community, and he discusses the role of the MENC Commission VIII—Music in the Community.

Music, Community and Social Change

PART 1

by Max Kaplan

I t is a sobering thought that only about eleven high school generations from now we will be in the year A.D. 2000. A good many graduates from our music schools in June of this year will be alive at that time, drinking through the night, or singing madrigals, or whatever sixty-seven-year-olds do on such an event. Had our graduates prepared to teach for Plato's academy in Athens, they should have been able to look ahead to only twenty-three years of life. Even as late as 1790, or twenty-one centuries later, the life expectancy was but twenty-four years. In 1850 it was up to forty. In 1900, forty-seven. But last year, each of our babies could look forward to sixty-nine years of life. And that, my friends, can add up to several million miles of vibrations coming out of durable French horns and double basses and pianos! It means that our students live more years, that we are around longer to work with them, but, fundamentally, it means that the world that has increased life expectancy in the past half-century more than

in all of the previous twenty-three centuries is a different world than the one that witnessed the beginnings of MENC. Our Golden Anniversary as an organization is more than a note in the passing of time. It is, indeed, a literal transition into a new kind of life, a new culture, and hence, a new teaching.

One need not belabor the obvious in recounting some major changes of this half-century. Hours of work went down steadily as technology and specialization took over. Vast populations moved off the farm, into the large city, then to the suburb. Several wars entered the picture. Government on all levels expanded. As a boy I listened incredulously to a crystal radio, with wires running around an oatmeal box; today, a finger motion operates an enormously complicated television set in my private home theater. As a boy, a trip of fifty miles was a memorable journey; today the average number of miles each of us travels between cities is 2,200 miles per year. A college degree is now the possession of millions. Our material comforts have shot up. Our health is better, And all this has had its effects on ideas, on the social structures of the family, place of worship, state, school, and community.

All together, it has been truly an era of fantastic change. Misery, comfort, maladjustments, strife, resettlement, new opportunities, personal adventure, emotional uprootedness, creative possibilities—all these have compounded into a kalei-

At the time this article was written, Max Kaplan was an assistant professor in the sociology and music departments at the University of Illinois. His current mailing address is Route 1, Box 108, State Highway 85, Senioa, GA 30276-9608. This article originally appeared in the September-October 1956 Music Educators Journal.

doscope of human drama whose depth can only be suggested by even the most penetrating of novelists, poets, or cultural philosophers.

For the world of music, this time has also implied changes of immense proportions in mass distribution techniques, in the training of many millions, in the growth of universities and colleges as creative centers, in the flowering of community amateur organizations, in new techniques of teaching, in dark economic days for the professional, in the growth of a strong union of musicians, in the migration of many European musical leaders from totalitarian nations, and in the impact of new organizations for the professional advancement of music, such as MENC itself.

Yet as we peer into the near future, these changes in the broad culture and in the arts as well, are only beginnings. We need not confiscate the Superman cartoons hidden in the desks of students for our glimpse. A more reliable source, in the form of sixteen volumes that resulted from the atomic energy conference of last summer in Geneva, provides our basic projection of energy potential. And this new energy is one significant clue to the new life, as indeed it is to the possibility of sudden death.

The unit of measurable energy to the scientists is the symbol "Q." Q represents the energy stored in 33,000 million tons of coal, or a million, million, million BTUs. In the eighteen and a half centuries after Christ, nine Q were used together, or one-half Q per century. Up to the seventeenth century, most of this energy came from human muscles, much of it from the work of slaves. Then came a wave of freedom from bondage to other people as well as from muscular work. By the year 1850, the use of tools and machines, as well as the expansion of life in general, led to the use of one Q per century, and by 1950 this proportionate consumption of energy had gone up to ten Q per century. Put in lay language, this means that today, in the United States, each of us has available and uses, every day, the same amount of energy as would in former days be created by a force of ninety slaves.

Atomic energy for peaceful uses can make even this look primitive. The best estimate of total recoverable world reserves of uranium and thorium is 1,700 Q of energy. This amount, even now available, is enough to take care of rising levels of life, a doubled population by the year 2,000. Its concreteness is already seen in power stations being built in the United States, Russia, France, and Canada.

Yet this revolution in the source of power—sooner or later to be perhaps eclipsed by solar energy—is half of the revolution. The other part consists of the new way in which power going into industrial plants and business establishments can now be controlled by electronic devices in the automaton techniques built around the factor of "feedback," or a form of self-correction and control. But I refrain from elaborating this second development, which for one of its implications has already done much to unify the A.F.L. and C.I.O.

These two revolutions—new power and new forms of control—are at the root of an emerging society whose consequences may, in time, reach into every human activity. They will, with the large social forces that led to them, affect types and hours of work, the nature of our goods and services, types of leisure activities, and concentrations of populations. Do not make the mistake of blandly ignoring this total picture and of assuming that art and music will be unaffected.

There are, I submit, only two ways in which the music teacher or the profession can approach this picture of social change. One is to ask, "What has this to do with me? Come atomic cars and walkie-talkies in every lapel, Beethoven will still be Beethoven. A fugue is still a fugue. 1700 Q? Any piano A will still be A440. Art has its own development—its own little revolution, perhaps, but are these not independent of social movements?" The following statement, made some years ago by Cecil Smith, then director of the University of Chicago music division, underscores that point of view in its attack on sociologists:

Perhaps the greatest threat to the restoration of music to a lofty position in the hierarchy of the liberal arts comes from the quarter of the social sciences. The half-science of sociology can do, and already has done inestimable harm to the study of music. Sociologists undertake to study human phenomena by means of data assembled in the same way that one would collect data about rocks or chemical elements. When they have gathered enough particulars, they add them all together into what they call social forces or movements, or they take an average and establish what they call a norm of social behavior or attitude. Then the process is reversed and these forces, movements, and norms are taken as causes of particular events. In music, it is very unsafe to talk of a particular composition as the result of a force; each piece of music is the very special product of one unique composer who sets out to propound and solve one unique problem.

This statement gratuitously gives sociologists more power than they deserve. The changes in society are not of their doing; the interrelationships of art and society are not of their creation.

A second approach, of course, is to seek an understanding of these relationships between art (a vital and integral function in society) and economic, political, social structures and tendencies. Once this is attempted, however, there is no stopping half way. All these facets and tendencies affect one another, and the ramification of this complex process cannot conveniently be ignored or talked away by the pomposities of cloistered musical scholars of today, as in earlier day by the Whistlers and the Clive Bells.

Let us assume the music teacher and musician of today is aware that, for example, the presence of war or peace does hold a connection to his or her work. Music teachers are certainly aware, on an everyday level, of the community in which their students, colleagues, bosses, audiences, and admirers live, work, play, vote, fight, or pray. Indeed, is there is not one of them who also—

perhaps outside of his or her role as musician— loves, prays, lives, and fights? What, therefore, is the relationship between these roles as musician or music teacher and as citizen, soldier, friend, fellow lodge member, Protestant, Republican, or spouse? Here again, two positions can be stated, although now there is an in-between possibility.

It can be held, on the one hand, that the music teacher's place is entirely in the school, and his or her assumptions are these: the nature of the musical art is that it is a separate, nonsocial tradition; the teacher is hired to do a good job in the school, not to dissipate energies elsewhere; in the normal course of events, he or she has sufficient contacts within the community, with parents, audiences, music stores, and others; he or she should not get involved in the tensions that often exist between factions of musical life in communities. Finally, perhaps most significant, he or she holds that a community should seek to develop its own resources with leaders from among its indigenous institutions; in this process, the music teacher may help, but should not usurp, limit, stifle, or discourage other sources of actual or potential leadership.

The opposite view might hold that the music teacher should be active in community artistic activities, relying on these assumptions: there are communities with a dearth of leadership, and little will be done unless the teacher steps in; art as an historical tradition has always moved into and between various social structures and forms, so that the music teacher, unlike teachers of many other subjects, belongs to the whole community; the effective music teacher must maintain close relations with all community resources, as in recreation, religious institutions, private teachers, newspapers, and so forth; his or her position in school work permits community leadership without involvement in squabbles. Most significant, from this view, is the argument that in many places there are few facilities for the high school music student after he gets out of school; if no one else does so, the teacher should help create such possibilities.

II

It is not the function of Commission VIII—Music in the Community to uphold one set of assumptions over the other. In actual situations, a variety of local factors as well as assumptions or choices by the teacher will influence one's course of action. It is our function as a commission, however, to articulate a philosophy of the roles of the music teacher in the community so that, given a specific local situation, the music teacher has at least been made aware of alternatives and implications and can act with a full awareness of the factors. One of these factors, for instance, is the nature of social changes in the community that may affect both the teacher's work in the classroom and his or her conceivable roles in the community—a change, for instance, in uses of the mass media.

Perhaps a second objective of Commission VIII might become that of addressing the community itself, to indicate the meaning and implications of such concepts as mass-oriented and local-oriented. Out of it might come suggestions on ways in which a community can develop a balance between the development of its unique values and advantages with the models or stimulation from regional and national factors coming into the home through publications, the airwaves, and recordings.

A third objective of the Commission is to provide a theoretical framework and a technique whereby the musical profession, untrained as it is in the social sciences, can still learn to know its community, to observe and assess its resources, and thus to create a more intelligent perspective of its own professional relationship to it.

Perhaps I may permit myself, even before such studies are undertaken by the Commission and collective conclusions are reached, the pleasure of several observations along such lines. I offer first some comments on evolving leisure patterns in our country, then some broad notes on trends in musical life.

It has been variously called the "new leisure" or "mass leisure." A report in the magazine *Business Week* for September 12, 1953, starts out, "Nothing quite like it has occurred before in world history. Never have so many people had so much time on their hands—with pay—as today in the United States." About twenty to forty billion dollars, perhaps about fifteen per cent of our total national spending, goes into leisure-time pursuits. More than a million workers are directly engaged in some enterprise related to such activities. Forty-two million American workers have paid vacations. The double pull has been in those activities that take us from our homes, such as domestic and international travel, and activities that keep us in or around the home, such as television, gardening, sewing, and do-it-yourself projects.

These tendencies may change in unpredictable directions. But these are facts grounded in a new technology, in a mobile society, with tastes and wants determined in part by Madison Avenue hucksters, with satisfactions coming from an ever-wider choice of ways for spending this new dimension of freedom—time. Their relations to music are not deeply hidden.

What does a greater range of leisure choice spell for the arts? What are the functions of music and art in such a transitory period? What is the musician's place in a philosophy of recreation? What new careers are now open to musicians, and what old jobs are closed? How do they find new roots, in keeping with the times, yet not surrendering their standards and theirs own need for aesthetic affirmation and values?

In part 2 of this two-part series of articles, Max Kaplan examines the possibility of a "wider function and social integration of music and art in a changing society." He analyzes community agencies of music instruction, production, distribution, and consumption and defines "community" as a multifaceted term that means different things in urban, suburban, rural, southern, western, and large and small locales.

Music, Community and Social Change

PART 2

by Max Kaplan

III

The world of music is a dynamic activity and process in this changing society. Although its directions are not always clear, its vitality is assured. There is a large amount of misinformation about the arts in America, a general ignorance about the ferment of artistic and musical activity on the community level. Much is heard about our many listeners, and perhaps there should have been no surprise when, during the memorable television showing of *Richard III* recently, Professor Baxter of California said that at that moment more people were watching than the total of all Shakespearean audiences since the play was written. It is true, however, that there is a cultural "explosion," as *Life* magazine has termed it, in the number of people who are themselves acting, painting, and making music as well as in the many millions

At the time this article was written, Max Kaplan was an assistant professor in the sociology and music departments at the University of Illinois. His current mailing address is Route 1, Box 108, State Highway 85, Senioa, GA 30276-9608. This article originally appeared in the November-December 1956 Music Educators Journal.

of youngsters who are being prepared in these fields for high levels of amateur activity. It was significant that last year, about five million dollars more were spent for concerts than for professional baseball. More important is the continued growth of almost a thousand community symphony orchestras in all parts of the United States.

Amateur activity has never been at a higher level of ability. In the field of models for performance, never has such an array of recordings been available at such modest cost. Never has the distribution of music been so far-reaching both by mass media and face-to-face. That more is not done is in part due to some of us who cannot reconcile industrial society with aesthetic and humanistic values. With this is the strong tendency, both among college musicians who inhabit past centuries by choice and among professional musicians whose economic base is weakened, to suspect this popular movement in the arts. They see in it a degradation, a lowering of standards. The standards they apply and the analysis they pretend are often built on the shaky structure of art as an aristocracy, talent as a rarity, mass media as a Frankenstein, and America itself as hopelessly pragmatic and noncreative.

The first requisite for us who should take the world of today and the astounding tomorrow into account is to rid ourselves of the platitudes that have cluttered our thinking about the arts for many decades. We are nation of many themes and values. We have the time now to be spectators and also to be participants in creative activities made possible by this new dimension of free time. The four hours each day, which we all have above that of our forebears of a century ago, is a period in which, our work having been done, the ends of life await our claim and our energy.

A task, therefore, of Commission VIII is to enlarge this phrase—Music in the Community—and to awaken MENC and the whole musical world to the real possibility of a wider function and social integration of music and art in the changing society.

IV

Several steps or phases can be outlined for this Commission in so bold and significant an undertaking. The first of these is to relate itself to other national agencies or systematic vehicles of thought about the arts. For instance, the American Music Conference has entered into a new concept of its functions and is considering how best it may serve adult activities in community music. The American Symphony Orchestra League has done a magnificent job in educating and supplying leadership to its member organizations. The University of Wisconsin has been a pioneer for several summers, bringing together men and women from the various arts to discuss a philosophy of creative community living, and to prepare themselves for more effective leadership. The Adult Education Association, at its 1955 meeting in St. Louis, held sessions for the first time on music in the community, and a committee was then appointed to continue this exploration of music and adult education. The Arts Center of Columbia University is even now preparing itself to serve as a national clearinghouse for community activities in all the arts, perhaps by such means as publications, clinics, and field consultants. Congressional hearings of importance were held in Washington last January and February on a variety of bills that would help

bring our art to European nations, make money available to state art programs, develop a permanent commission for the arts, and erect a fitting national center in Washington.

These are only some of the projects that point up the need for crystallization of national objectives, coordination, and unified action. With such groups, MENC can identify itself in part through Commission VIII. Thus, one of our objectives will be to maintain close relationships with such groups.

Within Commission VIII, several preliminary steps have been taken to establish a course of action or study. The first need was the formulation of a general point of view on the place of art in our society that would combine a positive stand on some issues with a reasonable social analysis. The opportunity for such a document came last winter when your Commission chairman was invited to present a series of thirteen lectures for the University of Illinois radio station. The series has now been issued in mimeographed form, and may later be published. This statement of about 125 pages, *Art in a Changing America*, will be submitted to all the members of the Commission and to officers of MENC as a possibly acceptable articulation of the problem in its largest perspective.

A second step came out of the conviction that while the Commission should and will collect and evaluate data and illustrations about music in community life, its constant aim should be to seek generalizations about music as a functioning theme or phenomenon in the community. Such an approach lends itself to criticism of those who want easy reading, simple clichés, or innocuous reports with pictures. Yet, only by providing some theoretical framework can fundamental principles be achieved. A later monograph, devoted entirely to the theory of music as the core of social process, will explore such areas as agencies of instruction, production, distribution, and consumption. Under each can be listed such agencies as the following:

Agencies of instruction: Adult education; conservatories and private teachers.

Agencies of production: Community orchestras and bands; choirs, choruses, opera groups; industrial units; professional groups such as the

American Federation of Musicians and the barbershoppers.

Agencies of distribution: Libraries; music stores, government; recreation departments.

Agencies of consumption: Clubs; homes; hospitals and other institutions; popular art; concert halls.

The question next arises, "What are some vital issues that face or might face the musician and music teacher in relation to each of these elements?" Such questions were therefore prepared, and are now in the hands of members of the Commission—about 175 questions in all. They were intended not to limit an individual or a committee, but, as a beginning, were merely to suggest some focus, or as the photographer might say, some "depth of field."

The next general problem is the nature of "community." When we speak of the relation of music or the teacher to the "home," to "professional groups," and so forth, much depends on whether we are talking about Oshkosh, Wisconsin, or New Orleans, Louisiana, a rural or an urban area, an industrial or a resort city, a slum area in Chicago or the Gold Coast. Quite aside from the normal accumulation of data that will come from a variety of communities, it will be of great advantage if we can stimulate several studies of total communities in order to observe specific variables that seem to come into play under given conditions.

The whole analysis as suggested, then, revolves around an understanding of those activities and agencies that explain a total musical-social scheme or process, and the isolation and specific study of variables that will help explain how and what happens under given conditions. At all times, such analysis must remain dynamic; that is, it cannot become a static picture that fails to take into account the many changes even now going on in American society or in its many types of communities.

What will be the nature of our society in the year A.D. 2,000 remains to be seen. Whatever its nature, your A will still be 440, but who will use that violin bow or the piano key, under what conditions of home life, within what patterns of leisure, through what context of community and nation—these matters will affect the musical functions, meanings, and indeed, the very presence of a musical life itself. To the extent that musical and artistic life in that atomic society is truly creative and significant, let it be recorded by our professional progeny, when it has sobered enough on January the 1st or 2nd, A.D. 2000, that we in the middle of the century were at least willing to look ahead of us and around us. Life then will perhaps be longer than our own; is it not our ultimate objective to make it increasingly richer and significant through the common heritage and possessions of the arts?

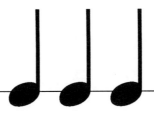

Section

The Individual and the Community

How does the individual citizen fit into the broad picture of music in our communities? Charles Leonhard gives an overview of the topic, and four other authors offer their ideas on the importance of amateurs—both individuals and groups—in keeping the arts community alive.

Americans have become passive consumers of the arts. Adults can counter the sterile mechanization and depersonalizing influences of contemporary society by participating in the arts, and arts teachers should work in the community toward this goal. The author describes a community arts education program whose participants gain a healthy sense of self.

People's Arts Programs: A New Context for Music Education

by Charles Leonhard

Walt Whitman's well-known poem "I Hear America Singing" establishes a rationale for a people's arts program. Whitman proclaimed that all men and women sing their own songs. He spoke of an America not limited by economic and social barriers, and his vision of America singing could be extrapolated to all of the arts. Along with Whitman, I believe that the arts are, for all people, an active avenue for expression, a symbol of life.

Even a cursory examination of the contemporary arts scene in the United States establishes the fact that this view of

civilization is far from fruition. Many forces in present-day society tend to broaden the chasm between ordinary experience and aesthetic experience. All the arts are generally relegated to a special place of limbo; it is a "higher" place, to be sure, but the higher the pedestal on which [the arts] are placed, the more remote they become from the everyday life of the people and the more average people will tend to disassociate themselves from art objects and experience. Music is relegated to the concert hall; the plastic arts, painting, and sculpture, to the museum. Even many devotees of the arts tend to compartmentalize their lives and think of their aesthetic experience as being apart from their ordinary experience. The average person is prone to consider the arts world a never-never land in which he or has little or no interest or stake, something so precious and strange that he or has

---

"I Hear America Singing"

I hear America singing, the varied carols I hear,
Those of mechanics, each one singing his as it should be, blithe and strong,
The carpenter singing his as he measures his plank or beam,
The mason singing his as he makes ready for work, or leaves off work,
The boatman singing what belongs to him on his boat,
    the deck-hand singing on the steamboat deck,
The shoemaker singing as he sits on his bench,
    the hatter singing as he stands,
The wood-cutter's song,
    the ploughboy's on his way in the morning,
    or at noon intermission or at sundown,
The delicious singing of the mother, or of the young wife at work,
    or of the girl sewing or washing,
Each singing what belongs to him or her and to none else,
The day what belongs to the day—
    at night the party of young fellows, robust, friendly,
Singing with open mouths their strong melodious songs.

—from Walt Whitman's *Leaves of Grass*

Charles Leonhard is professor of music education at the University of Illinois, Urbana-Champaign. This article originally appeared in the April 1980 Music Educators Journal.

no need for it. He or she thinks of art objects and art experience as being the sole property of a small, rather peculiar set of people of whom he or she is rather suspicious and whom he or she understands almost not at all.

This situation exists at a time when mass education in the arts, especially in music, serves to bring unprecedented numbers of people into contact with the arts, although the passing years have seen a steady decline in the amount of serious music on radio and television channels. The other arts only rarely appear in the mass media.

We have become victims of the isolation of art products from the human conditions under which they are created. I hold, with John Dewey, that "we must restore continuity between the refined and intensified forms of experience that are works of art and the everyday events, doings and sufferings that are universally recognized to constitute experience."[1]

Before the Tube

In earlier civilizations, aesthetic activities, objects, and ideas played a significant role in the life of the community. Everyday life was enhanced by a wide range of expressive activity. Household utensils and instruments for war and hunting were fashioned with extreme concern for the delight of the senses. Religious rites and celebrations were marked by dancing and pantomime. Drama, music, painting, sculpture, and architecture were closely woven into the fabric of everyday living.

In the early years of our own culture, aesthetic experience and ordinary experience had a close relationship. Harvest celebrations and frontier country square dances were shot through and through with aesthetic import. The singing school, the singing convention, and the family and group songfests that dominated the music life of an earlier day represented direct sources of aesthetic experience. None of these was remote from life nor were they considered effete or effeminate. On the contrary, they were vital, highly charged forces in the sentient life of the people.[2]

Social, economic, industrial, and artistic developments in the nineteenth and twentieth centuries brought about a disruption of this continuity between experience with the arts and ordinary experience. The increasing dichotomy between producers and consumers of the arts became a powerful force in this discontinuity. Huge orchestras played for huge audiences in upper-class European society. The roles of the amateur artist, musician, and composer were diminished to make way for the professional. As compositions exhibited ever-increasing complexity and the size of orchestras grew to accommodate the intentions of composers, producing music became a complex operation requiring a large crew of professionals presided over by the ultimate in professionalism—the conductor.

These orchestral establishments required vast amounts of money that could only be provided by huge audiences from the upper classes. The larger the budget, the larger the auditorium or concert hall had to be. A hundred musicians played for thousands of listeners. Professionalism resulted in high standard of performance, but the amateur became increasingly reluctant to compete with the professional. As a result, the devotee of music was pushed into a passive role; if he or she could afford it, he or she went to concerts to be entertained by professionals. The seeds of passive entertainment were sown and flourished in the mores of the people, not only in relation to music but also to theater, art, and dance. One redeeming feature, however, did remain: people had to make an effort to go to the concerts, plays, museums, and movies.

But then came television. A world of passive entertainment became available at the touch of an electrical switch. No longer did one even have to brave the weather or crowds of people to be entertained.

Television has become a shield from reality, an escape from the real world. Only the rich and a few intellectuals escape the tentacles of television. The rich ride their own horses, sail their own boats, and come into intimate contact with nature. Intellectuals read, reflect, imagine, and create.

The average American, on the other hand, watches television 1,500 hours each year, but rarely reads. The viewer's contact with the natural world is vicarious; his or her reflecting, imagining, and creating are packaged in ten-minute segments, with any continuity that exists being constantly broken by commercial messages.

Television has become a "sitter" for young and old alike, but it is an insidious sitter that inhibits interaction and involvement with other human beings. It provides a collective fantasy life that hinders the creation of our own fantasies.

Salvation through the arts

I view the arts as the only possible means to counter the sterility, the mechanization, the depersonalization, and the retreat into isolation that pervade contemporary society. The arts can play this role, however, only with a concentrated effort on the part of the arts community, public schools and colleges, and all levels of government to develop a true people's arts program—a program that will involve people at all levels of society in active participation in the art or arts of their choice, and a program based on the premise that the dichotomy between producer and consumer can be erased.

I view the arts as the only possible means to counter the sterility, the mechanization, the depersonalization, and the retreat into isolation that pervade society. The arts can play this role, however, only with a concentrated effort on the part of the arts community, public schools and colleges, and all levels of government to develop a true people's arts program.

I see the potential for every woman and man to become a producer of the arts—a performer, painter, sculptor, composer, dancer, or actor. I see a society that eradicates the chasm between ordinary experience and aesthetic experience and in which the arts become a part of the everyday life of the people, a society that demonstrates the continuity between works of art and everyday events, a society that no longer brooks the dichotomy between producers of the arts and consumers of the arts.

The arts again can fill for *all* people, not just the rich and privileged, the role of stimulating feelingful thought and thoughtful feeling, processes in which the imagination is freed, ignited, and takes flight. This freedom of imagination is what I believe to be the primary objective of experience and education in the arts. Today we have a plethora of feelingless thought and thoughtless feeling that represent the basis for most of the divisive and destructive forces in contemporary society.

The arts establishment in the United States is thriving. Support of the arts by government recently has become a matter of national policy. The appropriations for the National Endowment for the Arts have increased manyfold since its establishment. Diverse organizations are promoting the arts at all levels from national to local; the state arts councils, national arts associations, and the Alliance for Arts Education are only three of many. Fine orchestras dot the land, as do theater groups and museums of various sizes. A veritable explosion in dance has been generated at least partially by the well-publicized defections of ballet stars from the [former] Soviet Union, and American parents are no longer so reluctant to support a boy's interest in dance. Eight million people saw a recent PBS telecast of Verdi's *Otello*, an impressive event even in the face of the inevitable limitations inherent in the medium of television.

For many years, public-school programs in art and music have achieved impressive success in training the practitioners in those arts. Programs of substance in theater and dance have, however, been few in number. In recent years, numerous arts programs in the public schools have ceased to grow and thrive. Indeed, in many school districts, alarming cutbacks have occurred due to the difficult financial situation in which most public school systems find themselves.

Another factor of significance to school arts programs lies in the reduction of the number of school-age children and young people and the steady increase in the number of people beyond school age. With the projected decrease in the birthrate, the median age of our population promises to continue to increase. People will live longer and spend a growing number of years in retirement. Senior citizens now constitute a significant percentage of our population with growing political influence, and they are making increasing demands for social and economic programs that benefit them.

This combination of factors—the decrease in the school-age population, the increase in population beyond school age, and the growing difficulty that public schools face in financing a program of arts education—means that the time has come to broaden the clientele for arts programs to include young adults, people of middle age, and senior citizens. This expansion must be accompanied by a comparable broadening of the base of financial support to include not only school districts but also city, township, county, state, and federal governments; arts councils; park districts; and recreation commissions in cooperative sponsorship of a comprehensive arts education program designed to appeal to the interests and aspirations of the total American population.

Such a program would encompass performance activities, including bands, choruses, orchestras, small ensembles, folk-singing groups, dance groups, and theater groups; instruction in a variety of music instruments, including piano, guitar, recorder, and the traditional band and orchestra instruments; training in painting, crafts, sculpture, acting, and dance; and instruction and organized experience in listening to music and viewing art works and theatrical and dance productions. It would be funded by tax monies from school districts and other appropriate government agencies. Facilities would include school buildings, community centers, arts centers, senior citizens centers, and other public buildings.

Arts teachers would work in both school and community programs, either with joint appointments between the school and a community agency or with school district appointments partially funded by money from one or more other government agencies. The total program of school and community arts education would be coordinated and administered by a director with joint responsibility and authority.

Let us consider the shape and scope of a community arts program that provides access for every man, woman, and child, poor and rich alike, to arts instruction and arts experience. In a community with a school district, a recreation commission, and an arts council, the three agencies would cooperate in the support, development, and operation of the program. The music program would offer classroom music daily for children in kindergarten through grade 6, instruction in wind and stringed instruments in the fifth and sixth grades, general music in the seventh grade, and chorus, band, orchestra, and small vocal and instrumental ensembles in the middle or junior and senior high schools. This sequence would constitute a full program that seems increasingly beyond the resources of schools alone.

The school program also would include regular instruction in art production and appreciation, dance, and creative dramatics. Students would prepare and present art exhibitions, dance recitals, and plays.

The program for adults would offer class instruction in piano, guitar, stringed instruments, wind instruments, percussion instruments, painting, sculpture, crafts, dance, and acting for people of all ages, including senior citizens. Performance groups would include instrumental ensembles, vocal ensembles, male chorus, mixed chorus, women's chorus, folk-song groups using music from the heritage of ethnic groups in the community, barbershop quartets, dance groups, and theater groups. A community orchestra, band, dance group, and theater group would involve both school and adult performers. The performing groups would combine their resources for seasonal programs, community arts festivals, and theater presentations. The program also would provide instruction in music listening and composition and viewing of plastic arts, dance, and theater, along with trips to attend presentations by touring artists and performing organizations and exhibitions in museums.

The instructional team would consist of a director of arts with overall responsibility for the school and community programs and full- and part-time teachers, including wind-instrument, stringed-instrument, choral, and general music specialists and painters, sculptors, dancers, and actors, all of whom would teach and work in both school and community programs. Furthermore, community arts resources would be mobilized; residents with arts skills would be employed part-time to give instruction or conduct performance groups.

What are the advantages of such a program?

- The total community would have access to arts instruction and enriched experience with the arts through performance, study, and attending. All those yearnings that so many people have to learn to play an instrument, to paint, to sculpt, to act, and to dance, which now go unfulfilled, could be realized.
- The school would be enabled to have a full quota of skilled arts specialists it formerly was unable to afford.
- Unused arts resources within the community would be discovered and put to productive use.
- Arts teachers would be viewed not only as school arts leaders but as community arts leaders; they would become *of* the community and not merely *in* it.
- The program would serve to preserve the ethnic arts heritage characteristic of the community.

- Better understanding and enhanced appreciation of the total school program by the total community would ensue. Community members without children of school age (a growing segment of the population) would be more likely to support the school when receiving direct benefits from the arts program.
- Buildings and equipment of the school and community would be more fully used.
- The program would contribute to an enhanced sense of community unity and oneness, which has tended to disappear in the face of the extreme segmentation of contemporary living. Experiences shared by young and old would have a powerful unifying force that is largely absent in the nuclear family.
- The cultural and social life of the community would be enriched by the ennobling effect of experiencing the arts actively and directly. Leisure time would be used more constructively by both youngsters and adults as an alternative to shallow, tawdry pastimes or violence.
- All people, regardless of age, educational level, socioeconomic status, or race would have the opportunity to develop their ultimate humanity through enhancing their capacity for thoughtful feeling and feelingful thinking.

Is this a utopian dream? I believe not. It represents, on the contrary, a realistic response to the needs of people, a more efficient use of public and private monies already being spent, and an opportunity for all of the people to find true self-realization and insight into life values that are timeless, culturally significant, and personally satisfying.

Like Walt Whitman, I hear America singing.

The history of amateur musicians reveals that during the times when music was most highly regarded, amateurs played a major role in performing and composing. The current monopoly of professional musicians will probably give way eventually to a broader participation by amateurs. Music lovers need musical experiences that include both listening and performing—personal musical experience. Amateurs are critical to the creation and maintenance of a cultured society. We will have a truly musical community when amateur musicians have the musical opportunities they need to develop their musical interests and skills.

Amateurs and Music

by H e n r y   S .   D r i n k e r ,   J r.

A musical amateur is one whose interest and participation in music is prompted primarily by his or her love for music and by no ulterior consideration. "Professional" and "amateur" should not, musically speaking, be thought of as opposites. Even if a professional musician is one who earns a livelihood by music, he or she may be also an *amator* if his or her guiding motives are love for music and the desire to share his or her better understanding of it with others—if he or she is one of those rare souls who truly serve music, instead of expecting music to serve him or her. No one, on the other hand, is, in my opinion, a genuine amateur whose primary urge to make music is for the exhibition of a beautiful voice or a vocal or digital dexterity; nor, indeed, does such gymnastic proficiency constitute a musician.

Harry S. Drinker, Jr. (1880–1965), an attorney by profession, was a widely known pianist, composer, and author. He translated into English all the texts of the Bach cantatas as well as the complete vocal works of Brahms and Schumann. This article, based on Drinker's address at the North Central Music Educators Conference meeting in Indianapolis, Indiana, March 19, 1935, is reprinted from the 1925 Conference Yearbook. It also appeared in the September 1967 Music Educators Journal.

Delighting in Music

The word "amateur" is derived from the Latin *amator*, a lover, and is similar to the Italian *dilettante*, one who "delights" in music. As originally applied to the fine arts, these words did not carry their present connotation of superficiality. Dr. Burney, on his Italian trip of 1771, speaks of "Count Brühl, a great dilettante . . . who plays in a very masterly manner upon several instruments," and of the "famous dilettante, Count Benevento, a great performer on the violin and a good composer." In 1768, Boccherini dedicated his first string quartet *Ai Veri Cognoscitori e Dilettanti di Musica*—"To Those Who Truly Understand and Delight in Music"—an apt definition of a musician, whether professional or amateur. In our day, however, most musical amateurs are lacking in the understanding for which some participation in music and a great deal of knowledge of it is essential, and are thus unqualified to share in Bocherini's dedication. It was not always so. The time has been when amateurs occupied their proper place in the musical life of the community. It must be so again if we are to become a truly musical nation.

A few examples from music history will both illustrate the very different attitude of people in times past toward music and point the way to the reaction that I believe is soon coming.

Until the end of the seventeenth century, no one thought of asking people to come to a hall at an arbitrary hour to hear a "concert." Instead, musicians took music where music belonged: to the festivals, banquets, funerals, or religious services where the people were already assembled for some other purpose. The word "concert," spelled "consort," originally meant the group of performers; later, it came to mean the performance itself. Giorgione's picture, "The Concert," showing three performers, did not at all imply an audience outside the picture. These three players themselves constituted the "concert."

Part of Being Educated

The original aristocrats of amateur music were the troubadours and trouvères, from the root meaning to "delve into and discover," a significant hint for modern amateurs. These musicians were nobles, knights, and ladies. They not only wrote their songs but composed the music that formed an inseparable part of them. "A verse without music," said Folquet de Marseilles, "is a mill without water." The jongleurs and minstrels, the latter word being derived from the root meaning "servant," were mere professionals whom the troubadours hired to roam around the country singing and playing the songs composed and taught them by their noble patrons.

It is encouraging to Anglo-Saxon amateurs to read of our musical forebears in Elizabethan England. Elizabeth's father, Henry VIII, composed a whole church service as well as some thirty-three songs that his talented daughters doubtless sang with him and his successive wives. Of Henry in his younger days, Pasqualige, the Ambassador-extraordinary to Venice, thus reports to the Doge in 1515:

> He speaks French, English, and Latin and a little Italian, plays well on the lute and virginals, *sings from the book at sight*, draws the bow with greater strength than any man in England, and jousts marvelously. *Believe me*, he is in every respect a most accomplished prince.

The ladies of Elizabeth I's court were all able to accompany themselves and one another on the lute or other instruments. After dinner, the hostess produced the music books, and one who could not sing at sight was looked on as uneducated. A book of etiquette called *The Compleat Gentleman*, published by Henry Peacham in 1622, includes music among the necessary accomplishments, along with falconry, archery, and heraldry. "I desire no more in you," says the author, "than to sing your part sure and at first sight; withall to play the same upon your Violl, or the exercise of your lute, privately to yourself." In barbershops and waiting rooms (instead of today's salacious magazines), viols, citterns, and other musical instruments were provided for the diversion of the waiting customers.

The Decline of the Amateur

In England in those days, every music lover was a performer. Equally important, all were interested primarily in the beauty of the music, which skill in performance was only the means to bring out. What happened, however, was that the craze for part singing and the consequent competition in polyphony finally produced music that was overly difficult and complex, even for these sixteenth-century experts. There is a motet by Tallis, for instance, for eight choirs of five voices each—forty different voice parts.

At the beginning of the seventeenth century, there resulted a reaction to the solo, which made possible, during the next two hundred years, the rage for Italian opera. The musical pendulum now swung to the other extreme: people thinking only of the brilliance of the performer and scarcely at all of the beauty of the music. The artificiality of it all became unbelievable, culminating in those human calliopes, the castrati, whom an adoring public applauded as the singers trilled the part of Hercules or Agamemnon in highest soprano. By the end of the eighteenth century, all this artificiality and exaltation of virtuosity resulted in another significant reaction, and people were ready for Papa Haydn with his hearty Croatian folk tunes; for the melodies of Mozart, Weber, and Schubert, as fresh today as when they poured forth from those bottomless wells of melody; for the irresistible sincerity and power of Beethoven; and for the recognition of Bach, who in his own day was famous only as an organ virtuoso, and whose incomparable compositions were "discovered" by Mendelssohn eighty years after his death. There followed the Viennese period, when amateurs again took their proper place in musical life, the respected friends and companions in music of Haydn, Beethoven, Schubert, and later of Brahms.

Music:
A Participatory Activity

The significance of these brief references to musical history is twofold: first, they emphasize that the periods when music was soundly regarded were those in which amateurs took a major part; second, they show that the overemphasis of any phase of musical life causes a reaction to the other extreme. How, then, does this apply to our own day? Before attempting to answer this, we must consider the dominating characteristics of our present-day musical life. To do this is difficult, since we are in the middle of it.

Of one thing, however, I feel certain. The present monopoly of music making by the professionals cannot long prevail. The spirit of our age demands that everyone have a share in the desirable things of life. Here is one of life's choicest delights, in which everyone can have a part if he or she will only reach out a little to take it. Every normal child or young person (and most adults, for that matter) can learn to sing and to play a musical instrument just as readily and efficiently as he or she can learn to talk and to play games—some better, some worse, but all well enough to enjoy it thoroughly.

The idea that most people are born unmusical and that the making of music is but for the chosen few is a wholly false, though widespread, obsession, like witchcraft, hellfire, the idea that bleeding was good for sick people, or that tomatoes were not fit to eat. I am no more naturally musical than many of my supposedly nonmusical friends, but, thank God, I was exposed to good music when I was a child, and it took. There are no blue Monday mornings for one who goes back to work with a glorious Bach chorus rolling around inside his or her soul. Music thus actually experienced is more than amusement: it is a permanent addition to the spiritual life of the participant.

The Need for Musical Experience

The current unfortunate separation between professionals and amateurs has followed from the undue exaltation of brilliance in performance, which has gradually been raised from its proper function as a means for bringing out the beauty of the music to being constituted an end in itself. In deference to popular interest in performance, compositions have been made increasingly difficult, the professionals who have devoted their lives to mastering these difficulties have become scornful of any standard of performance inferior to their own, and the amateurs have little by little been discouraged and cowed into a condition of substantial passivity. An eminent musician, for whose musical judgment I have otherwise the most profound respect, recently expressed in public the opinion that the only proper role for amateurs in music is that of listeners. The professionals would thus monopolize the entire creative function of music, and turn us amateurs into mere musical eunuchs. God forbid! Although it is both vain and futile for amateurs to attempt to compete with professionals in virtuosity, no really intelligent listening to music is possible for one without personal musical experience. Furthermore, the musical understanding attainable by the participants in a reverent and enthusiastic, though technically inferior, performance of a masterpiece of music is far greater than that resulting from listening to a technically perfect rendering by others. Instead of a further separation between professionals and amateurs, what we should all hope and strive for is a merger of the qualifying members of each class into one, *musicians* all, according to their respective talents; participants, the less expert performers making up for their lack of skill by a broader and more thorough knowledge of music and of musical literature.

In my advocacy of active participation in the performance of music by amateurs as promising far greater pleasure and satisfaction than that obtainable vicariously by any amount of passive listening, I must not be understood as implying that listening to music is not a delightful and desirable form of entertainment, particularly when it takes the form that Schauffler happily characterizes as "creative listening"—when the audience brings itself into such intimate and hearty sympathy with the performers as to inspire them to a maximum response in creative effort. What is needed is not less listening, but more participation. As a supplement to participation, much intelligent listening is a necessary prerequisite to musical understanding. Undoubtedly, also, listening to music acts as a sort of spiritual massage, but, like physical massage, is much more effective and salutary after actual exercise and, of itself, will suffice only those spiritual invalids who vainly hope that substantial joy or satisfaction can ever come from any mere passive diversion, however soothing, to which they themselves offer no creative contribution.

The True Musical Society

Few people appreciate the function of amateurs in creating and maintaining a cultured society, or realize how much more essential they are than the professionals. To test this, let us imagine a genuinely musical community, abounding in those who "truly understand and delight in music," playing and singing, in their leisure hours, for their mutual pleasure and musical experience, and forming the intelligent audiences for an adequate group of professionals. If from this community all the professionals were forthwith eliminated, it would still remain a musical community; the amateurs would go right on with their music together, the only result being a temporary lull in a number of public concerts, until a new lot of professionals could be imported or developed. This would happen in a very few months, since the present supply of professionals throughout the country very largely exceeds the demand.

If, on the other hand, all amateurs should suddenly develop musical aphasia and amnesia, so that they were no longer able to sing and play or to discuss music intelligently, the community would forthwith cease to be a musical one, despite the professionals, and would so continue until a new group of amateurs could grow up, a process requiring not merely months, but years. During this period, the professionals would be compelled to lower their standards, both in the quality of programs and in the dignity and taste of their performances, to the level of their audiences, and they would be found playing and singing music that they thoroughly despised as the alternative to starvation. Those steadfast ones who were unwilling thus to debase their artistic ideals would move to other cities whose musical culture was sufficient to support them.

Music for amateurs will never amount to much as long as they continue to regard the giving of a concert as the sole goal of their musical existence.

Both of these results are readily observable today wherever the musical life of a community does not center around a strong nucleus of serious and intelligent amateurs. It is the amateurs in the community, not the professionals, who set the standards of taste in music and who are the ultimate arbiters of artistic achievement. While the professionals can do much toward maintaining and improving musical taste and standards, particularly by leavening and inspiring small groups of amateur performers, in the last analysis they will always be coerced into giving the public the kind of music and the type of performance that the public thinks it wants. It could not be otherwise; economic necessity corrupts good music.

Personal Musical Pleasure

What music lovers really want, although as yet many of them do not realize it, is the opportunity for personal musical experience. What they need is adequate, expert guidance and leadership in group music. The principal obstacle to attaining both is the prevalent obsession that the making of music is but for the chosen few, and that the purpose of a musical performance by amateurs is to give pleasure to an audience and to provide the performers with an opportunity to display their proficiency, whereas its real and worthwhile function is to provide enjoyment and intimate musical experience for the performers themselves. Music for amateurs will never amount to much as long as they continue to regard the giving of a concert as the sole goal of their musical existence. A beautiful voice or elaborate voice culture is no more necessary for the most intense pleasure and satisfaction from group singing than is the eloquence and training of an orator essential for delightful conversation. Certainly the average ballroom physique and posture do not indicate a similar attitude toward dancing, nor is it generally supposed than one must be a Luther Burbank to and enjoy one's own garden of flowers. Why cannot amateurs regard and enjoy their music in the same simple and straightforward way that they do golf, or bridge, or interesting books, or birdwatching, or the thousand and one other things that we do every day with no thought at all of attempting to show off or to compete with the expert?

Our lack of proportion in music is nowhere more pronounced than in the teaching of it. Would a teacher of English graduate a pupil who was unable to read a single new line of prose with intelligence and whose knowledge of literature was confined to the few poems or orations that the student could recite by heart? Although a few of the best music schools require their pupils to be musically well-rounded, the greater part of music teaching wholly ignores this common-sense requisite. Thus, a large part of the pupils who are not only accepted for vocal training but who afterward presume

to perform in public could not tell you the key they are singing in, and think that Monteverdi is a place in Italy.

Wanted: Leadership

What, then, is the moral of all this? It is that, except for a few geniuses, the future for those who desire to make their living from music is in the training of amateurs to participate in group music and in providing skilled leaders to enable the amateurs to make such group music interesting, successful, and really worthwhile.

Today, there is not only a need but an actual demand for such leaders, a demand about which the many unemployed musicians who still cling to the vain hope of giving concerts and studio teaching of individual pupils have no idea.

"The great field, the potential realm," says Dr. Keppel, "for providing continued excitement and thereby continued stimulation to the mature mind, is the realm of the arts."

Art is as broad as life itself, and no form of art can be confined within the limits of any class or group. The urge to personal expression through the arts, manifesting itself in the need to sing and play beautiful music, is fundamental and indestructible. Though it may lie dormant for a while, it will revive as surely as life returns in springtime. I look for a day, not long distant, when music will be recognized as an essential part of the daily lives of all cultured people; when mere dexterity will no longer be mistaken for musicianship or for musical understanding; when amateurs will again take their proper place in our musical life; when all true lovers of music—professionals, amateurs, performers, and listeners—will join in a renaissance of taste and understanding to make music the same fertile influence in normal life that it was in the days of our musical ancestors. In that Golden Age of Music, we will be able to claim a share in Boccherini's dedication: to be *Veri Cognoscitori e Dilettanti de Musica*— "Those Who Truly Understand and Delight in Music."

Max Kaplan defines the role of the musical amateur in the community and societal musical benefits available to this large group. The public schools can be credited with making so much music available in communities. The author presents five propositions to describe the amateur in American society.

The Social Role of the Amateur

by Max Kaplan

We can study the amateur only by talking at the same time about the professional. These terms, amateur and professional, are by no means opposites. Indeed, even a distinction between them offers difficulties. The most common difference usually considered is payment of money, while a second distinction sometimes used in differentiating amateur from professional is ability. A systematic analysis is required in order to bring these elements of payment for services and ability into some perspective. We begin by looking more closely at the concept of professionalism.

According to A. M. Carr-Saunders and P. A. Wilson, a profession is marked by "the possession of an intellectual technique acquired by special training."[1] E. T. Hiller goes farther, and speaks of five "variable attributes" of professions: (1) long, systematic preparation; (2) the presence of norms of conduct; (3) an "occupational conscience," that is, an emphasis on standards and services rather than material rewards; (4) recognition by the public of professional authority based on knowledge; and (5) a kind of personal bearing "consistent with the value served by the vocation."[2]

Max Kaplan formerly was an assistant professor in the departments of sociology and music at the University of Illinois, Urbana. His current mailing address is Route 1, Box 108, State Highway 85, Senioa, GA 30276-9608. This article originally appeared in the February-March 1954 Music Educators Journal.

Three Tasks of the Profession

The three tasks of the profession, according to an able analysis by another sociologist, Robert MacIver, revolve about maintaining its authority and prestige as a group, its "quest for new and better methods and processes," and its effort to spread the value itself, such as a love for art. But within this pattern arises the problem of reconciliation of interests caused by the attempt to "fulfill as completely as possible the primary service for which it stands while securing the legitimate economic interests of its members." A code of ethics, states MacIver, attempts to provide the solution, and thus becomes the characteristic and significant aspect of professionalism.[3]

With this background, we now put the professional and amateur side by side in terms of four elements or components of social role, namely, social circle, functions, status, and conception of the person. First, we have seen that professionals are accepted as such by their circle of patients, or clients, or audiences. He or she has authority because, like a police officer, he or she is simply delegated powers by the state. In addition, as Talcott Parsons notes, the relation of professional people to their clients or circle is impersonal, or as he puts it, "universalistic."[4]

Amateurs, on the other hand are not held up by their circles and can perform for whomever they wish. For instance, if you engage me, as a professional, to sing at your daughter's wedding, I will generally find out what you want sung, and when. As an amateur, I can sing on my own terms, turn you and your daughter down, or I can flex my vocal chords from 7:30 A.M. to 9:30

P.M.! Furthermore, since amateurs are dedicated to freedom, yet can enter into their activities with great enthusiasm, they can be expected to contribute new ideas. In this sense, the problem of every professional musician or artist is how to find a balance between freedom from his or her circle as an amateur in spirit at the same time that he or she is supported by it as a professional in occupation. The composer Mendelssohn put this dilemma into a delightful bit of doggerel:

> *If composers earnest are,*
> *Then we go to sleep;*
> *If they take a lively style,*
> *Then we vote them cheap;*
> *If the composition's long,*
> *Then its length we're fearing;*
> *If the writer makes it short,*
> *'Tisn't worth the hearing.*
> *If the work is plain and clear,*
> *Play it to some child;*
> *If its style should deeper be,*
> *Ah, the fellow's wild;*
> *Let a man do as he will,*
> *Still the critics fight;*
> *Therefore let him please himself,*
> *If he would do right.*

This issue of freedom is a burning one today—as it was in Mendelssohn's time—especially in the case of serious jazz players who seek to reconcile their love for real jazz against a flat pocketbook.

Second, consider function. The function of the professional is to make his or her special knowledge available, to serve, to uphold his or her traditions. The function of amateur activity is to recreate the person; if he or she performs for audiences or friends, it is for them to share his or her enthusiasm, not to serve or please a clientele. I recall the comment of a former colleague from the University of Colorado: "To the artist, the supreme form of applause is that coming from people who might have hissed him."[5] To this I add the paraphrase: "To the amateur, the supreme form of applause is that coming from people who might have kissed him." The amateur is not

to be treated or listened to as though he is a child; yet intense, mature, and serious as his effort may be, what the amateur does to art is less important than what art does to the amateur.

When we look, third, at status, or social rewards and returns that society provides to professionals and amateurs, a third comparison develops. The professional occupies a *key status* in his area of specialization. He or she is a professional lawyer, banker, or window washer. The banker or professor who collects stamps or looks at the constellations in the heavens at night is still the banker or the professor to society. His or her spouse is the spouse of a banker or professor, not of a philatelist or an astronomer.

Social and Economic Independence

Professional groups exist as formal associations, societies, guilds, or unions for two general purposes. Again, I use musicians as an example. The first union, or trade association, of this group was formed in 398 B.C. There is a record of a strike by this group fifty-seven years later, when the flute players were invited to perform at the four-day festival in the Temple of Jupiter. Since these proud musicians were not seated with the others at the banquets, but shunted to the kitchens, they called a strike, and even the athletes joined them until the bid for social equality was met. In the centuries that followed, musicians were sometimes loosely organized, sometimes (as in fourteenth-century France) a powerful body. Thus, to have established a *key role* as a professional means to be associated with a history for social as well as economic independence. Here is one aspect of struggle that professional artists feel and accept, even in our times, as a natural part of their careers. This is an aspect, needless to say, that the amateur is spared.

Finally, amateurs need not take the personal qualities that are associated with the activity they follow for pleasure. Yet there is more to it than social expectation. At least in the arts, the mind-life demanded of the creator is something distinctive. The point could be made in many ways. In reference to musicians, Virgil Thompson said:

No musician ever passes an average or normal infancy, with all that means of abundant physical exercise and a certain mental passivity. He must work very hard indeed to learn his musical matters and to train his hand, all in addition to his school work and his play life. I do not think he is necessarily overworked. I think rather that he is just more elaborately educated than his neighbors. But he does have a different life from theirs, an extra life; and he grows up ... to feel different from them on account of it ... musical training is long, elaborate, difficult, intense. Nobody who had it ever regrets it or forgets it. And it builds up in the heart of every musician a conviction that those who have had it are not only different from everybody else but definitely superior to most, and that all musicians together somehow form an idealistic society in the midst of a tawdry world.[5]

I have been comparing four aspects of professional and amateur roles: social circle, function, status, and conception of one person. These items, according to the eminent sociologist, Florian Znaniecki, constitute one's "social role."[7]

The Amateur in Fine Art

I proposed to limit my remarks to the amateur in some form of fine art, especially music, and raise the questions: What is happening to the amateur today in the United States? What do amateurs have to contribute? How are changes in the professional world affecting them? I approach these in a series of propositions.

I. *The amateur and the professional in the arts are not competitors, but close allies; their fate is interwoven.*

The community without both is barren. Each draws inspiration from the other: the amateur in order to learn and become more expert; the professional in order to catch the spirit of renewed zest for musical work. All of us, but especially the art amateur, is, therefore, concerned with the economic insecurity that befalls the professional today. In a recent radio address, I had occasion to illustrate this by the question "Must the Musician Eat?" Conversely, the professionals must always develop amateurs, for from their ranks come the most understanding of audiences. I also pointed to the record of the American Federation of Musicians in this regard, and took the position that this union, important through its function is, has seriously underestimated its reliance and its partnership with amateurs. To repeat, their fate is an interdependent one.

II. *In spite of current economic difficulties of professional artists, the amateur has never before in history had as many favorable social conditions as now in the United States.*

With the aid of mass media, amateurs can enjoy the very finest models, whether they be symphony orchestras, folksingers, or crooners. If amateurs write or paint, they have before them a revolution in the distribution of printing books and the reproduction of artworks. Furthermore, the present amateur can be anyone; he or she is not a dabbler who represents the upper classes or the aristocracy. Today amateurs play or paint because they enjoy it, and not to prove to themselves and others that they are free from obligation or productive work. Watch any of the several hundred community orchestras across our land and witness clerical staff, businesspeople, laborers, rich and poor, black and white, young and old, all playing side by side. Here is a result of middle-class ascendancy in the nineteenth century.

While music and the other arts still incorporate some sentiments and attitudes of feudal society, there is now a plain democracy of amateurism. I belong to an association of amateur musicians and have a list of members from the entire country; if I land in some Maine community with my violin and a member is listed there, I call on that person and we may play together. The application for membership does not ask my religion, politics, or family origins. From this type of creative fellowship in our own society arises a new challenge, for the same industrial conditions that enrich the amateur's life help to impoverish the professional. This challenge calls on amateurs to widen their horizons and to broaden their function from mere recreation to the making of art and music a communitywide activity. Amateurs have been helped already in this by an additional factor in American life, and this is my third proposition.

III. *Major credit for the favorable conditions now serving the amateur in art and music must go the public school system.*

We have in the schools many thousands of bands, orchestras, and choruses. A recent national sample showed that just about one out of every five of our more than forty-five million children under twenty years of age has learned to play an instrument. Howard Hanson, eminent composer, educator, and writer, noted a few years ago, "In the field of music education I think that the last fifty years have seen a progress in the United States which is so astonishing that we ourselves do not realize it. . . . Those of you who are old enough to recall what there was of music education fifty years ago, and now go about the United States hearing great symphony orchestras in high schools will, I think, agree with me that this is something that would have been considered almost unbelievable fifty years ago."[8]

Consider, furthermore, the tremendous amount of creativity and expression implanted among our school population in respect to writing, painting, woodworking, and a whole range of other avocational activities. The schools have long ago answered early arguments that the arts are frills. No one has put the issue more clearly than the philosopher, Irwin Edman: "Art, or the arts, adequately taught, are perhaps in our day the most central and important means of education. Far too long in American civilization the arts have been regarded as byproducts, luxuries, isolations and escapes. Far too long, in the Western world in general, education has been identified with the processes of the discursive, argumentative,

measuring and mathematical mind, breeding an almost superstitious exaltation of the laboratory methods."[9]

Yet, in spite of the gains made in the directions noted by Howard Hanson and justified in the words of Irwin Edman, there are greys as well as reds and blues in the picture. A fourth proposition, therefore, suggests itself.

IV. *Much of the potential for creative amateur activity is allowed to disappear after the school years.*

In some cases, the amateur musician, for example, finds no congenial company with whom to blow, fiddle, or sing. In others, adult life brings new responsibilities or different interests. It is also true that the expansion of commercial recreation has much to do in making listeners and watchers out of people who might make or do. Of course, there is much to be gained from radio and television, provided they fall into a balanced pattern of life.

The responsibility for providing creative opportunities for the amateur, I am convinced, belongs in part to the community. Over the past generation, a large responsibility has been accepted by American communities for providing recreational activities in games, sports, social dancing, and arts and crafts. Less has been done in the area of the arts. Even the school cannot reach into all phases of community art and music. For example, York, Pennsylvania, a city of fifty-six thousand, has fifty-six bands, fifty choral groups in addition to church choirs, thirty union dance bands, a symphony orchestra, more than a hundred Sunday-school orchestras, a ministers' chorus of sixty members, and bands formed by nine volunteer fire companies. The whole town, obviously, has somehow become involved, and beneath it there must be social structure and leadership that cut across school, occupational, and other institutional lines.

Here in Champaign-Urbana (Illinois) we have a new organization called Community Arts. Under one policy board, and supported only by contributions within the community, the past year has seen the formation of a symphony orchestra, a contemporary dance group, a massed chorus, a flute club, a string quartet, and painting and theater groups. Public and television appearances are made. A combined festival is planned for the spring. Already, amateurs in each of these areas have enlarged their circle, their function, and their status.

I come now to my last proposition, consisting of what to me is the ultimate distinction between amateur and professional:

> V. *The true artist, professional or amateur, is the person who struggles to be free of the provincial symbols and norms of his or her social milieu, while at the same time seeking to embody its deepest values into the forms and materials of his or her particular medium.*

"Genius," wrote Carl Merz in 1890, "lives in a world of its own," and in a real sense so does even the humble, sincere, artist whose achievements are much less. If, as Aristotle said, "no distinguished genius is free from madness," it is because no artist accepts society as it is; in practicing art he or she is continually remolding and reviewing it. The "madness," then, is not in him or her, but in his or her relationships with the followers, Philistines, or conformists. In this sense, all amateurs divide themselves: there are those who simply imitate, play at, and use art as therapy. No one can deny the validity of art as a recreational or therapeutic agent, especially in a gadget-minded and violent era. The greater amateur, however,

is the person who finds the opportunity for carrying out what, for him or her, results in a synthesis of life itself in its grandest significance. On this level of experience, the exalted amateur and the dedicated professional become one in their roles.

Notes

1. A. M. Carr-Saunders and P. A. Wilson, "Professions," *Encyclopedia of the Social Sciences.*

2. E. T. Hiller, *Social Relations and Structures,* Harper and Brothers, 1947, 544.

3. R. M. MacIver and C. H. Page, *Society, An Introductory Analysis,* Rinehart, 1949, 478-83.

4. Talcott Parsons, "The Professions and Social Structure," *Essays in Sociological Theory* (Free Press, 1949).

5. Paul-Louis Fay, "What a Humanist Sees in Music." *University of Colorado Bulletin,* XLI, no. 19 (November 1941).

6. Virgil Thompson, *The State of Music* (1939).

7. Florian Znaniecki, *American Journal of Sociology,* May 1939, "Social Groups as Products of Cooperating Individuals."

8. Howard Hanson, quoted by Harold C. Schonberg in the *New York Times,* 31 December, 1950.

9. Irwin Edman, quoted in the *New York Times,* 26 March, 1950.

In New York City, arts groups spring from neighborhoods and perform publicly. Support has come from foundations and government agencies for an opera company, a jazzmobile, a children's theater community workshop, a dance company, a symphony orchestra, a community theater, four Chinese festivals, and other participatory experiences. Community spirit is enhanced by participation in the arts, and by performing for friends and others in the community.

The Plasterer Plays Figaro

by Lawrence Locke

It is a hot night in New York's Bronx. Front stoops on 176th Street at Third Avenue, usually tiered with tenants escaping from their sweltering apartments, are empty. The sounds, too, are different. No car horns barking, backfires, tires squealing, or children shouting. Even the usual backdrop of casual talk and laughter has ceased.

Yet 176th Street is hardly quiet. People are sticking their heads out of windows, looking down on other residents who are encircling a small cluster of men. One of the men speaks, another replies, shouts erupt, then the residents roar. More heads poke out of kitchen windows, and people on fire escapes stomp, clap, and whistle.

Street fight? Accident? Riot? No—an audience. Noisy, irreverent, amused—a street theater audience. The play reaches an emotional peak in a revival meeting. An actor calls to his fellows to step forward and be saved. Deeply stirred, three old women step out of the crowd and into the play.

In Manhattan at the foot of Grand Street, cameras are filming a festival of music, dance, and theater that travels in New York's neighborhoods. The camera moves offstage and focuses

Lawrence Locke is a former staff writer for The Lamp, *a publication of Exxon Corporation. This article, copyright 1971 by Exxon Corporation, is reprinted from* The Lamp *by permission of the publisher. It appeared in the September 1972* Music Educators Journal.

on Inez Durand, 23, a slim, vibrant Puerto Rican who has just sung and danced in the street before hundreds of people.

"When I was dancing, I felt like everyone loved me," she says. "If I died at that moment, the whole world would be at half-mast."

The street play, Hazel Bryant's *Black Circles*, was being given a student production by the young actors of the street workshop of Manhattan's Negro Ensemble Company, a professional theater group. The traveling festival was the group Puerto Rico Sings doing *West Side Story*. They are just two of thousands of groups that are performing in the nation's neighborhoods. Spectators at these events often recognize a familiar neighborhood figure. Plasters become Figaros, bank tellers become dancers, and homemakers become divas.

A Smorgasbord of Offerings

Groups' memberships range from well-known professionals to the rankest amateur—and some have both. Generally, the more traditional and firmly structured arts, such as ballet, symphony, and opera, attract people who want to practice and perform with others equally accomplished. A second kind of group draws people, usually young, who aren't familiar with the arts. While these groups value artistic quality—and occasionally achieve it—the achievement is more of a means to personal growth than an end in itself. The third kind of group is a hybrid. Its members are practicing professionals who also conduct workshops for people interested, or even competent, in their particular art.

Regardless of whether the person holds the title, every group has a manager. In New York's Jazzmobile, it is Paul West, 36. West was a concert violinist until he came upon jazz in 1953. Several years after "really hearing jazz for the first time" in his life, West began playing bass for Dizzy Gillespie. He played until the early sixties, when he began laying plans for the Jazzmobile, a group that, like several others, has received help from corporations.

Steamfitters become kings, bank tellers become dancers, and homemakers become divas as the man next door and the lady down the block lend their talents to thousands of neighborhood arts groups.

As its name implies, the Jazzmobile is a vehicle that transports musicians—such as Duke Ellington, Gillespie, Charlie Mingus, and other top-ranking American jazz stylists—to concert sites. Playing on school grounds, squares, cul-de-sacs—anywhere a crowd can safely gather—the musicians give over one hundred free concerts a summer in Harlem and Brooklyn's Bedford-Stuyvesant section.

On a muggy August afternoon this summer, Duke Ellington and several other musicians appeared at 117th Street and A. Philip Randolph Square in Harlem. Newspaper notices had alerted the community so that before Ellington had struck the first key, one hundred people had surrounded the Jazzmobile. As Ellington played, the crowd grew.

Besides providing open-air concerts, the Jazzmobile runs a workshop for several dozen young neighborhood musicians. They meet on Saturdays in a Harlem school. West and the other professionals rehearse the students, who span the neighborhood social spectrum from Black Panthers to postal workers.

Performance is demanded. Criticism flows fast, laced with ribbing: "Man, you sure you're playing the same music we are?" from a teacher.

The Jazzmobile has had its dropouts and hangers-on, like any arts group. But a large number of the students never miss the Saturday rehearsals. The rehearsals are for the players' two annual concerts, which often give the students their first public exposure.

Building Self-Esteem

Musical success, however, is not the sole point of the workshops. "When a guy leaves here," says West, "he hasn't just learned how to play a horn or drums better. He's learned he can do something well if he bears down. That's what we want—fraternity, achievement, and the confidence that goes with them."

The students share West's attitude. "It involves you completely," says one. "I don't know what I'd do if the place wasn't there. It's like a home."

The Interboro Dance Company of Queens evokes a similar enthusiasm in its members. The company is small—twelve dancers, a costume person, a dance master, stage manager, and director—with a distinctly disciplined tone. All the dancers are professionals, dancing in such long-running Broadway musicals as *Applause* and *Promises, Promises*. With time out for Sundays and their matinees, the members rehearse for several hours daily.

"Our people are all master teachers," says Barbara Sedlar, the former singer who founded the company in 1969 and is its director. "They've been dancing for ten years. They came to the company to create their own works. Our aim is to support a permanent company of ten individual artists, rather than a small core of artists and a stable of dancers."

The dancers choreograph their original works, and the company performs them for varied audiences in Queens and elsewhere in New York City. During the summer, for instance, they performed at a retirement home in Far Rockaway, Queens. "We performed some quite sophisticated, satirical vignettes," says Mrs. Sedlar. "They loved it; they roared. We sometimes forget that people in old-age homes have lived lives.

"The works we create are positive," says Mrs. Sedlar. " They're serious. We're not encouraging Pollyanna fluff. But we feel optimism for life in this country, and we reflect this in our art."

Support from the Community

As in other cities, arts groups in New York have recently gotten help and encouragement from the business community. Corporations work through the New York Board of Trade, whose Arts and Business Cooperative Council brings together businesspeople and practicing New York artists—individuals and groups of all kinds—who need financial help or facilities to carry on their arts in the city. These arts may take conventional forms, such as opera, ballet, or theater, or less familiar ones, such as the Jazzmobile. Whatever the form, as long as they spring from artists in the neighborhood and draw an appreciative audience, the Arts and Business Cooperative Council considers them candidates for support by one of the Board of Trade's five hundred member corporations.

One example of support for these grass-roots artists was a $52,500 grant that Jersey Standard made last year as part of its broad, continuing program of support for the arts. The grant was made to the arts councils of New York's five boroughs. In presenting it, Clifford C. Garvin, Jr., an executive vice president of Jersey, noted that "the arts at all levels of a community are a unifying force which brings together young and old, rich and poor. . . . The ultimate proof of the viability of cities such as New York is the wealth of cultural activities being carried out in dozens of communities and neighborhoods."

The five borough arts councils sharing the grant have used most of it—a part has gone to sustain each council—to support performers in their bor-

oughs. In the Bronx, the Bronx Opera Company, composed of residents, benefitted. In Brooklyn, the money went to the Children's Theater Community Workshop, which helps youngsters create and perform their own works. In Queens, the Interboro Dance Company, the Queens Symphony Orchestra, the Queens Opera Association, and the Fresh Meadows Community Theater shared the funds. In Manhattan, Jersey's grant helped the Chinatown Planning Council stage four Chinese festivals, while in Harlem plans were laid for an exhibit and catalog of the work of the late Daniel Pressley, a Black sculptor. Finally, the Staten Island Council on the Arts used the funds to hire young people as tour guides in restored Richmondtown—the historic village first settled on Staten Island in the 1600s.

Jersey's interest in helping to encourage these spontaneous neighborhood arts, as well as the established arts, is simple. Several years ago, the company committed itself to keeping its headquarters in New York City, where its new office building is being completed. In making the decision to stay in the city, rather than leave for a surrounding suburban town, the company became familiar with the many urban problems provoked by size, density, and the desire for a higher quality of life.

One way to improve that quality, the company concluded, is through the arts, which can bring people together and refresh them. This is as true, of course, in the neighborhoods as it is on Broadway perhaps more so. So Jersey chose to supplement its support of established museums and theaters by contributing to the neighborhood arts.

Jersey expects, as Mr. Garvin said in his presentation remarks, that the neighborhood arts especially will "tap the constructive, creative energies of people, as opposed to the destructive instincts which drive men apart."

Sometimes we lose sight of the real value of musical participation for many community members, including those who enjoy performing chamber music. They do not aspire to becoming professional musicians, nor do most have enough talent to go beyond amateur status. Amateur community musicians value the joy of firsthand experience, but are often not trained adequately to be independent performers. Independence, of course, is a fundamental characteristic of effective chamber musicians. Generally, music educators should remember that they are preparing future adult amateur performers whose educational needs are somewhat different from those of future professionals.

A Chamber Group on Every Block

by L. Legrand Anderson

A friend of mine who loves to sing attended a choir rehearsal recently. The choir president and the director spent a lot of time discussing ideas for building the reputation of the choir through travel and recordings. My friend was disappointed. Once a week she wanted to stop being a wife and mother and become a singer in search of the joy in music; she didn't care whether the choir went anywhere or not. She felt guilty for not being as eager as the other members to build the choir, but the important thing to her was her weekly creative effort.

I wondered then, and I still wonder now, what's wrong with singing for the joy of music? What's wrong with being a musical amateur? As music educators, we go to great lengths to develop in our performing groups a "professional" attitude. We train our instrumentalists as though playing with a symphony orchestra were the highest goal possible. We train our singers toward the goals of recitals and opera; we encourage them to sing in competitions and auditions. Many directors of performing organizations strive for the "highest

professional standards." They wants their musicians to be "professional" in all senses of the word, regardless of the participants' desire or talent.

The Dependent Student

Perhaps our most regrettable fault is that we train musicians to be dependent on a conductor. Students become so accustomed to being pushed toward professionalism that they can't guide themselves through any music. Their performance practices are weakened, and they are unable to "figure out" a piece of music. We seldom give students an opportunity to work in small ensembles, and when we do, they expect the teacher to find the music to be played, to give tempos, to describe stylistic practices, to tell them, in short, "how it goes." They never learn to make music *by* themselves and *for* themselves, which are marks of a good amateur musician. This definition of an amateur does not lessen the technical demands and the musical understanding that can be gained from study. Rather, it changes the emphasis from performance to self-direction.

Why do we teach people to be professional musicians when they have only desire or talent enough to be amateurs? Why do some musicians, at least in their minds, look down on the amateur? Perhaps it is because we are so defensive about our poor muse that we feel everyone must want to strive to be a great musician, professional in

L. Legrand Anderson taught vocal music and theory at Granite High School, Salt Lake City, Utah. This article originally appeared in the May 1972 Music Educators Journal.

attitude if not in fact. Perhaps it is because music is so important to us that we can't bear to see it be merely a hobby to someone else. But is it not enough that music brings joy? One of the reasons that music education is in trouble may be the emphasis, from secondary schools through college, on musical training aimed toward professionalism—and especially professionalism in the area of performance.

One positive result of the American music education system is that many of the neighbors on any block have at some time had something to do with music in school. But most of them have long since sold their violin or saxophone or haven't sung a note in years. Many studies have examined the significant loss of interest in music between high school and college and the tremendous loss after college. Most studies mention such reasons as lack of time, but it may be that these people quit music because they didn't know how to be amateurs. Perhaps they simply didn't know what to do without the forceful guidance of a conductor to lean on. It's not much fun to play the third trumpet part without the rest of the band. But if we could develop amateur musicians properly, chamber groups on every block could be organized—not just the standard string quartets or piano trios, but all conceivable combinations of instruments. The purpose of these groups could be to make music by and for themselves.

Creating Independent Amateurs

We music educators should spend more time on music fundamentals with an eye toward independence for the student and less time on performance with an eye toward glory for ourselves. To achieve this, let's teach our students to sight-read not just proficiently but fluently. They start learning to read the printed word in the first grade. If they spent even a small fraction of that amount of time learning to read music, they would be superb readers. Instrumentalists usually learn to read more proficiently than vocalists or pianists. The technique of most pianists far surpasses their ability to read music; as a result, few pianists ever have the thrill of playing in an ensemble. I know two pianists of moderate skill and talent whose vocations lie in other areas but who get such tremendous gratification from reading four-handed piano music that they often go without meals to read a new piece. When they find new music, their excitement is like an antique-lover who finds a major treasure for $1.95. To sight-read—to explore a different world with a different language—is an exhilarating experience. It is unfortunate that the door to this language is closed to many musicians.

The demand for professional musicians is not great, and the competition is fierce. Almost every college has music majors who the faculty knows full well should have another major. These students usually have no burning desire but come to music because they enjoy it or because they had a high school music teacher who inspired them. They should be amateurs, not music educators—especially now that the supply of teachers is growing far faster than the demand.

Rediscovering the Joy of Music

Music educators say they are trying to make music available to the masses, yet I sometimes wonder about the desire of the masses for music. Consider the weeks of rehearsal, the hard work, and then the disappointment when the hall isn't filled. Chamber music concerts or vocal recitals are scheduled in immense halls that are inappropriate for these intimate arts. Symphony orchestras are dying for lack of audiences. People just don't go to concerts. But amateur musicians don't need audiences; they can perform music simply for their own enjoyment.

There is a joy in music that comes only to the performer: the joy of recreation. If we begin teaching students to be self-directing amateur musicians, perhaps they will rediscover that joy in their own music.

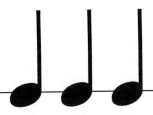

Section

Widening the Circle

In making the case for arts education, it is no longer enough merely to have your superintendent's support; community group and individual involvement are essential. In this section, music educators expand their influence beyond the schools.

Gene C. Wenner proposes ways in which arts educators and community leaders and artists can work together to strengthen and improve school arts programs. Assistance from the community can help decide not only the nature of the arts curricula and level of financial support, but even whether there will be viable arts programs in the schools. If the community is to help the schools, then arts educators must participate in the community. Wenner offers several suggestions for how arts educators can help enrich their communities with their unique talents and skills.

Joining Forces with the Arts Community

by Gene C. Wenner

Although public support for the arts has dramatically improved in recent years, support for arts education programs has not kept pace. I have spent many years working at local, state, and federal levels to build bonds between schools and communities, and, after all this time, I am convinced that music educators must work with the arts community to create appropriate arts education curricula. Unfortunately, there are many barriers that currently stand between schools and arts communities. One of the largest obstacles is that arts educators and arts administrators do not understand each other's rules of governance, goals, and resources.

A Little Background

A closer examination of the arts community might be helpful when addressing the question of cooperation. The establishment of the National Endowment for the Arts in 1965 served as the major impetus behind the recent growth in support for artistic organizations. Before that time, a few major symphony orchestras and opera companies were successful in raising support on their own,

Gene C. Wenner is an arts consultant in Reston, Virginia. He formerly was special assistant in the arts to the United States Commissioner of Education. This article was originally published in the December 1988 Music Educators Journal.

but they were located only in major metropolitan areas. Today arts organizations exist and thrive in both suburban and rural communities, serve millions of patrons each year, and provide greater employment opportunities for musicians.

In funding the Endowment, Congress wanted to encourage the establishment of state arts councils. Although their numbers were severely limited in 1965, these councils are at work in every state today. To help boost the councils, the Endowment provided funds to state arts agencies with the provision that they must match the money dollar for dollar. Each state then had to pass legislation to provide that matching support. Today, because of that initial plan, every state legislature appropriates more funding for the arts than the Endowment supplies. Although these funds are designed to support the work of artists, arts organizations, and local arts agencies, there is nothing in any state charter that requires the support of arts education.

The arts community, then, was developed from the top down (national to local), and state arts agencies have become increasingly successful in obtaining yearly increases from their legislatures. The same state legislatures that provide funds for arts agencies also allocate money for schools, yet lawmakers rarely make any connection between the two. One legislative committee typically grants funds to arts councils while a different one is concerned with education. Of the monies allocated for education, the majority are based only on student population and go directly to local school districts. Generally, no specific funds are set aside for arts education because legislators assume that the districts will continue to support it.

A few states have passed separate legislation to support arts education, but this practice is rare. In 1984, the National Conference of State Legislators reported that although twenty-two states had passed legislation defining arts education as part of basic curricula, these same legislatures did not fund those courses. At that time, fourteen states required arts education training for certifying classroom teachers, but usually required the completion of only one course. As of 1988, twenty-nine states had enacted high school graduation requirements that in some way include the arts; forty-two states required arts instruction at the elementary and secondary level.[1]

A Question of Support

With this increased interest in the arts, why haven't the schools done more in arts education? Although it is obvious that declining school populations, the emphasis on special and vocational education, and the ever-present "back to basics" movement have all played a part, a closer look will reveal that something more insidious is at work. For the past ten to fifteen years, many school districts have eliminated the major elements essential to arts programs: district supervisors and in-service arts training.[2] Teachers' meetings at the district level are still held once or twice a year, but they concentrate mostly on performance schedules and rarely on curriculum.

Because of this situation, arts teachers have become isolated from each other and from other school concerns such as scheduling, counseling, and budgeting. Another effect is that the music program becomes disjointed, and students do not receive a sequential, coordinated arts education. This policy also places arts educators under the supervision of principals who may or may not understand the importance of a high-quality arts program and who believe that elementary classroom teachers should be able to teach all subjects, including art, music, dance, and theater. Although some classroom teachers are trained in the arts, the majority have no background in and little commitment to teaching the arts.

The Buck Stops Where?

Who decides the fate of arts education in individual schools? In the past, the superintendent and his or her staff made most of the decisions and passed them down to the district music supervisor. The supervisor then would oversee the implementation of those decisions. In today's educational system, most decisions are reached through a process of mediation or accommodation involving school boards, teachers' unions, special-interest groups, parents, principals, and sometimes antischool groups interested only in lowering taxes.

In making the case for arts education, it is no longer enough merely to have the superintendent's support; community group and individual involvement are essential. Fortunately, the number of administrators, teachers, parents, and artists rallying in support of arts education is growing, but arts educators must persist to meet their goals. It is not enough to attend one school board meeting or to speak with administrators occasionally. Arts educators must continually be present and visible in the educational decision-making arena. Groups that support arts programs must be present at key meetings of parent-teacher associations, teacher's unions, and special-interest educational groups to be certain that the interests of arts education, and particularly music education, are served.

There is much that music educators can do to further their goals. Music teachers have often chosen to isolate themselves from other teachers, from curriculum or school meetings, and from parents' groups. Class schedules can also foster isolation since music teachers must teach so many classes (some of which are even in different schools). In spite of these limiting factors, many courageous music educators have been able to achieve their goals. They have only managed to overcome the isolation, however, through significant sacrifice and dedication. Those words are not very popular in today's educational climate, but going beyond the normal call of duty often is essential in establishing a sound music program.

An Agenda for Change

How, then can music educators use the swell of support for arts in the community to help make the case for their music programs? The relationship between arts organizations and schools has historically been an aloof one. Administrators of and performers in arts organizations generally do not understand the problems of music educators and do not, in many instances, know how music functions within the larger educational system. Music educators have not been very effective in explaining their roles and how the arts community might best assist them.

One of the primary areas in which general misunderstanding and distrust exists is in artists-in-residence programs. State and local arts councils typically believe that the only answer to a music program's problems is to add a few artists; obviously, this is not the ultimate answer. Schools and artists can be vital partners, but not without first observing the following principles of successful partnerships:

1. An artist must be ready to work with the school to develop support for the existing music education program.

2. Discussion sessions between an artist-in-residence and students can provide positive and educational results. It is important for children to discover both that artists are normal human beings and that their art is approachable. Artists who work in schools need careful planning, skill in working with children, and a flexible approach.

3. The artist-in-residence has to do more than just get students excited about music: He or she also has a duty to get classroom and music teachers involved. The artist should go to various teachers, find out what they are doing in their classrooms, and then relate his or her sessions to those topics. This "teacher-centered" approach requires a great deal of flexibility and planning

time. Unfortunately, state arts agencies and school districts seldom provide this time.

This cooperative effort can produce an extremely successful program in which children learn things about themselves, artists, their environment, and, above all, the arts. In current partnerships, performance is often overemphasized, and little time is spent on creation. Musical composition, choreography, and playwriting should be as important as playing, dancing, or acting. Although many of the artists and arts agencies that currently provide services to schools have increasingly tried to meet these criteria, it is up to the schools to insist that these programs measure up to their standards. Making more effective use of arts resources must be part of any comprehensive, sequential music program: This means teachers and administrators should build a program, then use community resources to expand and improve on it. Changes in attitudes toward the arts and in existing programs do not simply occur by adding another set of courses, hiring another specialist, or bringing in a few artists: They are the result of cooperative planning, careful implementation, and persistence.[3]

Arts Advocacy

Another area in which the arts community can build support for the music program is in the political arena. "Advocacy" is in vogue now: The word implies that "outsiders" (artists, arts organizations, and other interested parties) should help "insiders" (teachers and administrators) by advocating more arts programs in the schools. Because an outside voice can be very persuasive in the mediation-accommodation climate of school management, in certain situations advocacy makes a great deal of sense. Advocacy becomes a problem, however, when what the outsiders advocate is not what the insiders need. This can set the stage for an antagonistic relationship.

Although advocacy is a polite word for lobbying, the advocate is often not willing to lobby, instead choosing to keep a proper distance when school boards meet on critical arts decisions or when legislatures are passing laws that are damaging to arts education. The arts community should lobby the legislature on behalf of arts education separately from their own arts advocacy efforts. Arts educators, who should assist the arts community, have been woefully inadequate in the orchestration of efforts to turn advocacy into action.

Professional education associations like MENC, the National Arts Education Association, the National Dance Association, and the American Association of Theater for Youth are active in the promotion of K-12 programs in their respective arts areas. New interest in arts education also has appeared recently at the national level in the National Endowment for the Arts and the American Council for the Arts. In 1985, the Endowment changed its program name from Artists in Schools to Arts in Education. Since then, it has developed pilot programs for state arts agencies to collaborate with state and local education agencies.[4] There is help available, but the battle can only be waged effectively at the local and state levels.

Reforming Attitudes

Music is a legitimate area of study, and there is undoubtedly more interest in arts education today than ever before. It is up to music educators, however, to capitalize on this potential support and direct the flow of interest toward improving, expanding, and strengthening music education. Here are some suggestions for bringing the arts community into your school:

1. Ask influential members of the community to support your program by appearing at school board meetings when critical decisions are debated. Ask them to write letters on behalf of the music program to administrators, school board members, and state legislators particularly when critical issues that affect arts education are being debated.

2. Search for individuals who might be able and willing to talk about an area in which you have little expertise. You might be surprised how many people would be pleased to participate in such a class.

3. With the help of the arts community, develop a comprehensive, long-range plan for K-12 sequential music programs that it will support. Do not assume that the community understands your hopes for the program, let alone what you do every day in the classroom.

4. Invite the arts community to the school to observe your teaching and the students' learning processes: These are your best "sales tools." Be sure that the emphasis is on learning and not performance.

5. Take your classroom (not just your performing groups or exhibits) into the community. Find opportunities to show examples of classroom activities or rehearsals to the school board or the boards of local arts organizations so they can see firsthand what actually happens in schools.

6. Finally, you must be active in the politics and activities of schools and arts communities outside your own district or interests. Speak on behalf of your local or state arts agency when possible, or become a board member of a community or state arts agency. You cannot expect community groups and arts agencies to work on behalf of music education programs unless you are willing to reciprocate by working for all arts programs.

All of this may seem like a lot to ask. To settle for anything less, however, will result in an isolated music program that stays conveniently hidden in the music room and ultimately may disappear from view altogether. Build for tomorrow, and build on the base of support that the arts community can provide. It will be more than worth the effort —and your students deserve nothing less.

Notes

1. *Arts Education and the States* (Washington, DC: Council of Chief State School Officers, 1985).

2. Charles Fowler, "Opportunities for Cooperative Efforts," in *Arts and Education Handbook: Guide to Productive Collaborations* (Washington, DC: National Association of State Arts Agencies, 1988), 19-22.

3. Gene C. Wenner, "Why Would Anyone with Money Want to Give It to Arts Education?" *Design for Arts Education*, March-April 1987, 28-29.

4. *Toward Civilization: A Report on Arts Education* (Washington, DC: National Endowment for the Arts, 1988), 19.

Edward Sparling recommends that music teachers be trained to develop comprehensive music programs so the greatest possible number of students will participate actively by singing or playing instruments. This upbeat article urges music educators to find ways to get as many people, both in the school and the community, to participate in music. Sparling poses the question "How, you may ask, does one hitch one's wagon to the musical star of the masses?" He counters this first question with another, namely, "What is stopping you?"

Music for the Masses

by Edward J. Sparling

The statement could be made and substantiated to a considerable extent that there is not a school in our whole country, elementary, secondary, or collegiate, that has anything resembling a comprehensive music program. Of course, some music educators think that they know of a comprehensive all-school music program, and some may believe that they preside over or participate in such a program, but there would still be those who would be convinced without the aid of supporting data that such programs are not adequate for "music for the masses."

Only in the past two or three decades has the well-trained music teacher appeared in our school systems, especially in the elementary schools. Traditionally, music is still taught by the teacher who knows little music and for the most part has poor powers of inspiring the young to joyful participation in vocal and instrumental music. A few of the suburban and larger city systems have a special music teacher for a school, and at times a single school will have both choral and instrumental instructors, but even in the best schools

Edward J. Sparling is the former president of Roosevelt University, Chicago, Illinois. This article, taken from the author's edited manuscript of an address originally given in Chicago at a meeting of the Music Educators National Conference, appeared in the November-December 1956 Music Educators Journal.

the great majority of the elementary pupils arrive at graduation with little or no vocal training, and a very small percentage has been able to participate in the school orchestras and bands.

Expanding Music Experiences

In a high school with the most comprehensive music programs that it has been my privilege to observe, only one student in four participates in the choral societies, orchestras, and band. At best, three-quarters of the students of this school have to obtain most of their enjoyment of music by listening to others participate. It is my conviction that participation in vocal and instrumental music activity is more beneficial and developmental for the individual than is the more passive activity of listening, however enjoyable that may be. The training of the voice and instrumental instruction enhance the powers of appreciation for music.

It is my hope that the music teachers of today can extend music instruction to far greater numbers than ever before. Perhaps one of the best ways to show what can be done is to cite a few instances of people untrained as teachers of music who have brought joy to hundreds through the transfer of their enthusiasm for music.

Many years ago in California, I visited a roommate with whom I had attended college. My visit was enhanced by the performance of an orchestra that he had formed for the young people of his neighborhood. His interest had grown out of the inspiration caught from a retired first clarinetist of Sousa's Band. Coming to a city of twenty thousand, speaking very little English but strong in his enthusiasm for good music, this Italian musician gathered around him hundreds of young people. He formed a band of nearly one hundred pieces, and within two years he had not only developed an outstanding first band but had seven stand-ins for each place in the band. Hundreds of townspeople and farmers with their families from miles around attended his concerts, given twice each week. At the beginning of his third year of "retirement" he was made instructor of music for all the public schools of the city from kindergarten through the junior college. While a member of Sousa's Band, this man never had taught music, yet in retirement he taught hundreds and brought homemade, live music to the masses of one town in California. He shared fully what he had to give—a love for and a joy in the production of music—and his influence grew in ever-widening circles in and about his city of retirement.

Just as everyone who can move his or her muscles can be taught to swim and enjoy it, so everyone who has vocal chords with which to produce sounds can be taught to sing.

Another example of an enthusiasm for sharing musical experience, which grew like the tree in the heart of Brooklyn, is that of a young boy who at the age of twelve visited a mental hospital with his mother. The agonizing cries of the hopelessly insane ringing in the corridors impelled him to want to do something to prevent insanity. For six years he spent his weekends reading all the books he could find on the subject of insanity. In those books he ran across the oft-repeated statement that those who participated regularly in musical activity were less prone to insanity than others. The minister of his church, on the boy's request, allowed him to form two choirs, junior and intermediate. Although he had not had formal musical training previously, his choirs gained acclaim for the quality of their performances. He studied religious music for its contribution to the development of personality and then went on to become a distinguished professor in a leading New York medical school.

Benefits of a Universal Approach

The reason for telling of this musical interlude in the life of a musical amateur is the hope that some music teachers may be inspired by the purpose of that Brooklyn boy to hitch their wagons to the musical star of the masses. How, you may ask, does one hitch one's wagon to the musical star of the masses? This question could be countered with another, namely, "What is stopping you?" The answer is that "you and you alone are stopping you. The only reason you are not reaching the masses is that you are not aiming to bring musical experience to all within your reach."

Perhaps I can clarify my reasoning by drawing on my experience in teaching the physical sport of swimming. In assuming the task of teaching swimming in a high school of 600 students in California, I determined that everyone should know how to swim. If this was to be done with greatest dispatch it would be necessary to organize large classes for group instruction. In a comparatively short time all the students were swimming, and this provided large numbers from which to choose a swimming team. However, no team was chosen as such. The whole student body—the mass—was the squad, and each student had the opportunity to try out two days before each swimming meet. The team was created by the stop watch—the two boys making the fastest time in each event were the school representatives on the four school teams.

With every boy having the opportunity to make the team, the development of all was phenomenal. The teams formed in this manner regularly defeated schools with four to six thousand students to draw from. The failure of the larger schools to develop their best possible teams was due to their failure to adopt systems of training for all of their students. The system they used was to establish a squad of twenty or thirty members and these were the trainees. With this system they never found but a few of their potentially great swimmers. Those with hidden potential who could not swim or who swam poorly when the squad was formed were never found. The most important point to note here is not that the school had winning teams, but that several hundred young people learned to swim, learned how to protect themselves in the water, and learned how to enjoy themselves in a healthful, constructive sport that would enhance the quality of their physical activity throughout their lives. The winning teams were the natural outcome of the development of all, which included the best and the poorest.

Having followed through on this system of instruction for all, there is one inescapable conclusion, and that is no one can determine the development potential of any one individual until the individual has had training. Some of the most unlikely-looking prospects before training in swimming were some of the best after training. The greatest good of such a system of instruction is the constructive, healthful, and enjoyable sport added to the program for the benefit of all students. The winning team is a concomitant dividend issuing from the broad base of instruction for all.

The parallel that I wish to draw has significance for music for the masses. Just as everyone who can move his or her muscles can be taught to swim and enjoy it, so everyone who has vocal chords with which to produce sounds can be taught to sing. Among ten people who are taught to swim, there is at least one person with great potential for form, speed, and endurance. Similarly, it can follow that among ten people who may be taught to sing there is one person who has considerable potential ability for exceptional vocal performance. Those with voices of great quality can only be found by training everyone. Through continued training the great will emerge.

These analogies would seem to put the emphasis on finding the great or producing a winning team or a superb glee club, but this is not the case,

because the level of instruction and the joy of engaging in musical expression will be enhanced for all. Music of, by, and for the masses will produce the superb and the sublime.

Extending Instruction to All

Again the eternal question arises: How can we possibly give voice instruction or even choral direction with our limited budgets? In answering this question, of one this we can be certain: There can never be instruction for all until those responsible for instruction determine to reach all. This is impossible of accomplishment in a large school without the extension of instruction through those who have been taught to teach. Advanced students can be taught to form groups throughout our campuses. From these groups formed in clubs, dormitories, and classes, other groups can be formed for stepped-up and higher-quality performance.

By cherishing the idea of universal participation for all people within your institutions, are you as a teacher of music being impractical? My own answer to this question is: you are being most practical by reaching all with some type of musical training, even though you had no greater ambition for your services than to turn out a superb choral group or an outstanding orchestra. Your greatest chance for outstanding achievement is to have your performing groups emerge from the training of the greatest numbers it is possible to train.

Genuine greatness is not likely to be achieved by teachers who looks on their work as a duty rather than a privilege, as a job rather than a service, or as second-best to the concert stage. Teaching of music is a noble profession. But the one that is greatest among you must be the servant of all. If you hitch your wagon to the star of the masses and if your students catch the gleam of service through music in your eye, the masses will receive at least some training in music, and your country will be peopled by masses of singing, playing, happier human beings.

Family participation in music study is an old and proven concept that music educators need to appreciate. Concerts that are structured to please all members of the family provide a way of enjoying music not normally available in concerts for single-age groups. Family concerts are a way of celebrating togetherness.

Musical Togetherness: Creating Concerts for Families

by Nell J. Sins

This is probably not the kind of concert scene with which you are familiar: A baritone is singing the story of "The Green-Eyed Dragon." Near the end of the song, a "real" dragon walks in behind the singer who, oblivious to its presence, sings on. Audience children shout with laughter as the performer discovers the object of his song.

This scene is from a successful series of concerts for families presented by the University of South Carolina (Columbia) School of Music over the past four years. Any music club, school district, or university can organize these concerts. Every community and university has a rich mine of resource people—musicians, dancers, actors—to call upon. Here are some guidelines.

Use an Intimate Facility

The children should feel close to the performers, so the use of a stage is inappropriate. A cafetorium or even a gymnasium is more appropriate than a standard auditorium. A raked seating arrangement

Nell J. Sins is an associate professor of music education at the University of South Carolina, Columbia, and, at the time this article was first published, was the coordinator of the family concert series there. This article originally appeared in the November 1986 Music Educators Journal.

with the performing area at a lower level works well. This setting permits performers to relate closely to the audience members and even to move among them.

Keep It Short

There are usually toddlers present, and parents appreciate a program that is not so lengthy that they have to leave before the end. Fifty minutes seems to be a good length. A rule of thumb is that individual performance pieces should not exceed five minutes.

Performers must be tolerant of the fact that young children squirm and sometimes "can't wait." The value to these children of exposure to a live concert far outweighs the need of the performer for rapt silence. This does not mean, however, that children cannot be taught the advantages of concert manners before the program begins.

The concert segments can be tied together through the comments of the host of hostess. It is preferable that each performer make informal comments about the instrument or composition, but when a musician or dancer feels awkward about doing this, the host can step in and provide interesting facts. The host should relate well to children and not speak above their heads. The host can also explain concert manners in a congenial way (sometimes parents are unaware of these niceties).

Animals and Critters

The Bird and the Beast . . . . Celius Dougherty
The Lemon-Colored Dodo . . . . (Mezzo-soprano) . . . . Irving Mopper
Poisson d'or (The Goldfish) . . . . (Piano) . . . . Claude Debussy
The Wood Nymph (Nightingale)
                                  (Soprano and Renaissance instruments) . . Thomas Arne
The Green-Eyed Dragon . . . . (Baritone) . . . . Wolseley Thomas
The Nightingale from "Elizabeth Rogers Hir
Virginall Booke" . . . . Louis-Claude Daquin
Le Coucou (The Cuckoo)
La Poule (The Hen) . . . .(Harpsichord). . . . . . . Jean-Philippe Rameau
I Bought Me a Cat . . . . Aaron Copland
The Flea . . . . (Baritone) . . . . Ludwig van Beethoven

Figure 1.

Inject Some Humor

Each concert should contain at least one occasion for high jinks. Parents and grandparents enjoy a good laugh as much as their children. Furthermore, a humorous happening can be turned into a learning experience. In one of our family concerts, a horn player came out with a length of garden hose that he proceeded to play with a brass mouthpiece. After a short argument with the host, who insisted this was too undignified, the horn player retreated behind the sound shells, where much hammering was heard. He then emerged with a horn! This was his opportunity to explain how many feet of tubing it takes to construct a horn.

If a woodwind quintet is present, the players can have an instrument-disassembling contest, letting the children guess which instruments come apart into the most pieces.

Include Local Dancers

Choreography can be useful in giving exposure to original compositions by faculty or student composers. Audience members who have difficulty listening to electronic compositions will sit fascinated as the music is being danced. Faculty dancers and their students thrive on the challenge of choreographing such music.

Choreography can also enhance performances of established compositions. For example, "Beauty and the Beast" by Maurice Ravel can be performed by duo-pianists and dancer or actors.

Have a Theme

A theme can provide eye-catching material for press releases and can also serve as a source of ideas for publicity pictures. Figure 1 shows a program with the theme "Animals and Critters."

Other ideas for themes include "April Fool," "Music's Moods," and "Composers Have a Sense of Humor." For the latter, music selections could include "I Hate Music," by Leonard Bernstein, "The Cat Duet," by Gioacchino Rossini, "Opus Number Zoo" for woodwind quintet by Luciano Berio, and "Golliwogg's Cakewalk," by Claude Debussy. Figure 2 shows a handout and a list of pieces for a "Hold the Phone!" program.

Involve the Audience

The children can be given concert-related crossword puzzles (figure 3) or find-the-word games as they enter, receiving hints from the host as the program progresses. The audience can sing a simple song, led by the host and accompanied by one of the performers. For instance, a professor of electronic music had the audience learn a short, seemingly nonsensical song that he recorded. When he played the tape backward, the children and parents delighted in hearing themselves sing "Merrily We Roll Along."

Children love to shake the hands of costumed performers as they leave. This is a time for conversations and questions. The families are invited to examine instruments of interest and to ask questions of the individual performers.

Why Have Family Concerts?

Shinichi Suzuki long ago recognized the importance of family participation in music study. The philosophy of many early-learning schools now is to involve parents more in the learning experiences of the children. Family concerts expand on this idea by presenting the message, "It is a normal thing on a Sunday afternoon for a family to attend a concert together." The concerts, which mix lighthearted music with serious music and combine humor with some down-to-earth learning experiences, are often appreciated as much by the parents as by the children. When young, precocious children are included as part of the concert, parents recognize musical potential.

Families often see themselves as individuals—as parents leaving for work and children going to school. Our next family concert will consist almost entirely of family groups performing—*celebrating* together. The families attending this concert will be, in their own way, celebrating, too.

Hold the Phone

PHONO   A combining form meaning *sound, voice, speech, or tone.*

Find these words: sousaphone   xylophone   saxophone   vibraphone
                           telephone   phonograph   metallophone

```
L  I  S  T  E  N  A  P  H  O  N  O  G  R  A  P  H  O
G  E  T  S  A  X  O  P  H  O  N  E  T  O  D  A  Y  U
M  E  T  A  L  L  O  P  H  O  N  E  S  I  N  G  S  A
H  I  S  X  Y  L  O  P  H  O  N  E  M  A  L  L  E  T
M  Y  V  I  B  R  A  P  H  O  N  E  M  U  S  I  C  C
O  N  S  O  U  S  A  P  H  O  N  E  L  O  U  D  E  R
H  I  S  T  E  L  E  P  H  O  N  E  N  U  M  B  E  R
```

Suite for Young Listeners   Fred Weber
   (One movement)   Saxophones

The Elephant Dance   Fred Weber
                          Vibraphone
Phoney Business   —
                 Metallophones, Xylophones
Phonograph
[An old Edison record, demonstrated on an early wind-up phonograph]
   Aria from The Telephone   Gian Carlo Menotti

Figure 2.

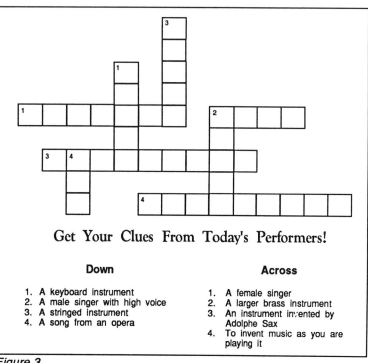

Get Your Clues From Today's Performers!

Down

1. A keyboard instrument
2. A male singer with high voice
3. A stringed instrument
4. A song from an opera

Across

1. A female singer
2. A larger brass instrument
3. An instrument invented by Adolphe Sax
4. To invent music as you are playing it

Figure 3.

Musical performers should structure their performances in such a way that they are more understandable and accessible to the public. Music educators can help make the community more receptive to the arts by offering well-balanced programs, helping prepare audiences for what they are about to hear, and by working to make musical experiences available to graduates of music education programs. Special attention must be paid to educating parents and other adults in the community, whose ability to listen and appreciate can assure the health of music in the community.

Take Music into the Community

by Robert E. Bliss

Everyone is concerned and everyone blames the public—that uncultured, illiterate mass of people who would rather hear Tom Jones than Robert Merrill. Of course the public is to blame. We in the arts are working diligently to bring them good music and getting little or no response. Besides, it is easier to place the blame on a mass of nameless people than to point an accusing finger at ourselves and our colleagues. The fact is, though, that this is where the greatest fault lies. Many performers show poor attitudes toward their audiences and some show outright contempt; management does little to keep ticket costs in line with the dollars available; music teachers frequently fail to develop a sense of respect for the art in their students and in the community. Music educators can do little to directly affect the first two failings, but they can improve music education.

Ask yourself as a music teacher what you have done to make your own community more receptive to the arts. If your answer indicates that you offer an outstanding band, orchestra, or chorus program, that your concerts are well-balanced presentations

Robert E. Bliss was an assistant professor of music education and a coordinator of the Division of Continuing Education, University of Missouri–Kansas City. This article originally appeared in the October 1971 Music Educators Journal.

of serious and light music, that the young people who work with you seem to like you and to enjoy what they are doing, that the parents of your students constantly tell you how amazed they are at how well the kids play or sing, and that you bring back many honors from music festivals and marching competitions, then you really do very little. These are only the first steps in what needs to be done to enrich the cultural life of a community. The problem is that most teachers never get beyond the first steps. They teach their classes well, as those who preceded them taught well; but consider the status of the performing arts in America.

More than Great Performances

Music educators are neglecting a major responsibility when a young person can graduate from the school music program, never again to be involved in music. He or she may have learned to read music well, to blow well, and to take eight steps in every five yards on the football field, but this knowledge will have little influence on his or her adult musical behavior. The student's parents came to school concerts to *see* their child on stage; as long as the band started and stopped together, did not play too far out of tune, and looked good, the parents were not concerned about the musical content of the course or concert.

What can be done to take music into the community? There are no easy answers, but teachers must begin now to think about the problem. First consider one basic premise: music education must be directed toward more than producing outstanding performing groups. Of course, it is one thing to make such a "profound" statement and another to know what you mean by it and how to help others understand it.

There are many meanings that could be attached to this brash proposition, but the one intended concerns the need to communicate the many joys of music to an entire populace and not just the one joy of fine performance to a small group of youngsters. Complete fulfillment in musical experience comes from a triangular relationship and communication among composer, performer, and audience. The audience and performer can be one and the same—surely the performer must always be his or her own audience, in part—but most likely the audience involves more than the performer. What teacher must do, then, is to help performers become good audiences, and this is done by teaching them to listen well, not only to their own music making, but to the music making of others. Educators must also direct some of their energies toward the development of nonparticipating members of the community as potential audiences. The development of good listeners is no doubt the most important function that music educators can perform, as it is in this realm that those who come under a teacher's influence will have the greatest opportunity for long-term participation.

If we are to make a lasting impression on the cultural life of our communities, we must teach the parents as well as the children.

Involving Adults

If we are to make a lasting impression on the cultural life of our communities, we must teach the parents as well as the children. Parents' nights, when mommas and papas are invited to listen to the results of a semester's activities, and open houses when parents visit with teachers and question

them are both fine educational tools but are highly limited. These are really only methods of getting the parents' permission for student participation. They help to make the parents aware of the goals for their children, but they do nothing to involve the parents in music or to assist them in gaining aesthetic experiences of their own.

The point, of course, is continuing education in music, and there are more opportunities for service in this field than there are teachers to go around. Efforts in adult education will create a more supportive constituency, brought about by their greater understanding, which will help provide the additional resources needed for all aspects of the school music program. An individualized program must be designed for each district, but there are some standard ideas than can form a basis for program development.

A listening course for adults can be offered, but it had better not be the dried-up "music appreciation" course that has so often been the standard fare. The teacher must be very secure in his or her subject matter, because the mature and analytical minds of adults offer real challenges to any instructor. In this line, one could offer a class similar to a college foundation course in music without the extensive reading assignments and the testing program. Since music educators should really be concerned with more than music, a team-teaching, interdisciplinary approach to the arts might be considered. Adult groups are highly responsive to a general cultural survey course dealing with the social background and social implications of the arts and the relationships between the various art forms. In addition to serving as a basic introductory course to the arts, such an approach may help adults to identify areas of specific interest to them, which will lead to the establishment of further course work in program planning. An interdisciplinary approach may also result in opportunities for mixed-media productions in the regular school program.

Supporting Local Music Activities

It is well to be reminded of the teacher's responsibility to support arts programs outside the public school. In many cities of various sizes, performance series are presented that may bring recitalists, chamber music programs, theater, and even major orchestras to the community. Certainly, musicians and teachers will be ticket holders and regular attenders, but they should also take an active role in the organization and administration of these programs. The music teacher might well be asked, and expected, to serve as part of a committee selecting the programs for a series, as publicity or ticket chairman, or in any other active capacity. It is vitally important that all music educators become involved in the programs of their community and that they promote these activities on behalf of their own students.

Music making should not be overlooked as an area of interest to parents and members of the community at large. People do enjoy and learn from the applied-music approach. There is the possibility that a mother or father might be interested in learning an instrument along with the child when he or she is enrolled in band or orchestra. Perhaps there could be a parallel program in music for the parents with beginning, intermediate, and advanced band for these adults. Such an approach might develop a communitywide musical organization of tre-

mendous stature in the future, which would serve not only to fulfill the personal needs for making music but also as an inspiration for the participants to enjoy the many other opportunities in music that come their way.

Using Available Resources

The community at large presents a problem or area of concern that easily and most often slips out of focus in the busy-ness of our daily schedules. Surely the goal of every music teacher, drama teacher, literature teacher, and art teacher is to affect the society in which he or she lives by making people more aware of the arts and by better equipping them to understand and enjoy the arts.

A few ideas have been presented here, but there are many resources for assistance in programming, such as the National Adult Education Association and its state affiliates, extension and continuing education divisions of state and private universities, and the adult education programs of the many Jewish Community Centers in most major cities. Teachers who contact one or more of these resource institutions and begin a program of adult education will be rewarded with a community that is responsible to and supportive of the school music program.

This group of brief contributions to MEJ is aimed at using community musical resources for school music programs. The ideas are valuable because they can help students experience the musical life and work with the musicians of the community. Suggestions are included for helping students take advantage of community concerts by Marilyn Sassman, for older students to assist music teachers by Richard R. Maag, for using films for vicarious arts experiences by Alice Levine, for apprenticing with instrument craftspeople by James D. Craig, and for using local musicians in the classroom by Reginald T. Buckner. Other contributors include Janet F. Ban on use for bulletin boards, Robert Henly Woody and Jane Divita Woody on using mental health professionals, and Peter B. Oliver on getting help at all levels, including national organizations.

Idea Bank:
Using Community Resources

Students Earn Points with Cultural Events

Too many times there is a missing link between the listening lessons we give in school and the concert halls where live music is performed. I have instituted a method called the "Culture Club" to encourage sixth-grade students to attend music events in the community. If they attend a symphony concert or another concert in or around the community, they can earn fifty points. They can also earn fifty points by going to any concert at the local university as well, and these performances are often free. Film musicals or stage plays earn forty-five points; high school concerts, thirty-five points; junior high concerts, twenty-five points; and other elementary concerts, twenty points. Rock concerts are not included because rock is the music best known by students. The most points are earned for attending concerts of the least familiar kinds of music. An added incentive to attending high school and junior high concerts is that it may increase the students' motivation to continue with music groups.

This "Idea Bank" originally appeared in the January 1977 Music Educators Journal.

The goal of the club is to see how many students can earn 100 points during the school year. In the past, almost fifty percent of the students have reached that level. There are no prizes as such—just the reward of having found a new kind of music resource. In most cases, it is a pleasurable one. A student's grade is not adversely affected if he does not go to concerts. Those who do go, however, usually find the added experience makes them better students, and, consequently, their grades improve.

The bookwork is easy. After students have been to a concert, they fill out a form in our room with their name, the event they attended, and their opinion of it. I then record points on a class chart so they can easily see how they are doing.

I have further tried to increase the contact between students and performing artists in the following ways. Once a couple of college students who were part of an opera came to our school to perform a portion of it. Advertising it through the club greatly helped to encourage students to attend. Another time I prepared a slide show and tape about a college professor who had built his own Viennese pianoforte an was scheduled to give a concert on it. The slide presentation helped to advertise the concert, and, as a result, several students attended the event.

I also interviewed the conductor of the local symphony and played the resulting tape for the students. I put up a monthly calendar, listing cultural events to attend, where and when they are, and how much they cost. Students seem to enjoy the opportunity to grow culturally and discover new events in the community. It also give us a greater chance to discuss these events in class and share them with others.—*Marilyn Sassman, music teacher, Rice Elementary School, Des Moines, Iowa*

Right in Your Own Backyard

One community resource is often, surprisingly, overlooked—music educators. It is always easier to look to others to give, but what of giving ourselves?

There are numerous opportunities to use services within our own profession. If there is a nearby college with a music education program, why not ask an interested student to help with a special project or tutoring? College students are more career-minded than ever and would relish the opportunity to work inside a school with a professional. Such an undertaking could also give the prospective music educator an opportunity to work in a field that might be different from his or her special interest. An instrumental music education major might work in an elementary general music class, or an elementary music education major could help in the production of a high school musical.

High school students who are interested in music could help with middle school or elementary music programs. This is common in other subjects in which older students tutor younger ones in reading or mathematics. Older students can help younger ones in learning the skills involved in the study of music concepts.

Undoubtedly there will be organizational problems in the sharing of administrative responsibilities between the professional music educator and the helper or apprentice. The rewards of a better and more personalized music education program,

however, are well worth the effort.—*Richard R. Maag, Furman University, Greenville, South Carolina*

Using Films as Team Teachers

The successful teacher of general music must be a first-rate performer, a clear lecturer, an incisive thinker, and at times a magician. Without these talents, it would be impossible to stage a daily show for today's required music class.

This term, I have two Westinghouse scholars in a fifty-student class alongside ninth graders with low reading levels. It is a mixed bag—each pupil having unique abilities and music preferences. The biggest problem, however, is not class size or student differences; it is our competition—television, radio, and recordings. How can we expect to compete with these media?

Perhaps our chances would be better if we were able to offer our classes a visit to Madrid's Prado for a Zabaleta performance, or a trip to the Spoleto music festival to see Menotti rehearse and perform Debussy's *Pelléas et Mélisande*. If only we could take students to New Orleans to view the opera, the jazz museum, and the Preservation Hall Jazz Band, or to San Francisco to hear ancient Chinese music or to see an "electronic ballet." In the past, such trips would have been impossible, but now your class can have all this on color films. There are excellent films available: the Mormon Tabernacle Choir singing *Messiah* in an outdoor amphitheater in the Rocky Mountains, a Toscanini commemorative; a visit with the Casadesus family; and many more.

For some films, I provide names of performers, compositions, and composers on the chalkboard. When the names are spoken in the film I turn on the lights briefly to allow students to see the names on the board. Occasionally I will turn down the sound to give explanations if the narrator is difficult to understand or if his or her meaning is unclear.

These films provide experiences that few of our students will ever have outside the classroom, so you may want the class to examine them closely. Familiarity with the films can allow you to prepare the class for more difficult listening experiences. With some classes I turn down the sound briefly and read the words to a recitative or aria. Before sections containing art songs, I call attention to some aspect of vocal production or to the different demands of art and pop songs. I ask the class to notice such things as the use of facial expression in transmitting meaning to the audience. If building vocabulary is one of your aims, the films can be helpful in introducing or reinforcing musical terms.

If you prefer more traditional assignments, each student can be made responsible for specific information on each film. If, instead, you prefer a more innovative approach, these films can be a resource for unlimited class discussion or committee research. Students in my classes have been stimulated to produce slide projects on the Lincoln Center, music in nearby colleges, and our own chorus trips.

Regardless of your particular interests or attitudes toward teaching music, you will find these films richly instructive, and often available on free loan.—*Alice Levine, music department, Cardozo High School, Bayside, New York*

Interning with Instrument Craftsmen

While our schools do an admirable job of introducing students to music performance, history, theory, and composition, they are rarely concerned with the building and maintenance of instruments. Many means to this end exist using various resource people and facilities.

A "Music-Electronic Technician Program" (MET) would provide the student with experience in maintenance, repair, and building of electronic instruments and audio equipment. Existing departments, such as music, sciences, shops, and audiovisual, should cooperate with a local repairperson acting as adviser or instructor in a club or class situation. The district administration, in conference with the repairperson and cooperating departments, could determine the physical logistics of the program with regard to its continuation through the grades.

The program would take place on three levels. In the elementary school, students would learn the use of basic mechanical and electrical construction tools, building simple kits, such as low-power amplifiers, preamps, audio oscillators, and radio tuner circuits. Basic circuit tests and the use of the analog volt-ohmmeter would be introduced. In the middle school, students would build intermediate kits, with emphasis on more complex test procedures and building tools to make these tests. There would be an introduction to digital electronics. Kits built might include a digital volt-amp-ohmmeter, digital frequency counter, and oscilloscope. In high school, students could begin to troubleshoot and repair the school's audio equipment and electronic instruments under the repairperson's supervision. Digital electronics should be widely explored, with emphasis on integrated circuits and logic circuitry. Advanced kits might produce a digital radio tuner, synthesizer, electronic organ, or microcomputer. Throughout the program, creative experimenters should have the opportunity to "breadboard" their ideas. Even limited exposure to MET should provide a student with the basic skills to repair patch cords or replace switches, while full exposure should result in great proficiency at repair.

A "Violin-Maker's Apprentice Program" would be similar to a vocational-technical school work program. Students would be selected for possible apprenticeship to a local craftsman and learn and work in his or her shop. Early stages could be devoted to the study of materials (woods, varnishes, glue) and an introduction to the tools and processes of violin making and repair. Apprentices should spend at least one-half day a week at the shop toward the end of their high school years, with their training culminating in the production of some finished instruments and the development of good repair techniques.

Most students instinctually accept and are influenced by technology—especially in communications—although few can make it work for them. But someone who sees a computer program he or she created running successfully surely feels, if only for a moment, in control of his or her fate.—*James D. Craig, owner, James Craig Music, Allentown, Pennsylvania*

A Posting Place

In a large metropolitan area that supports a major symphony orchestra, opera, and ballet, has several universities with music departments, sponsors concert series that bring noted soloists and ensembles into town, and draws popular groups to its music halls, there are many opportunities to hear the best in live music. Similarly, there are many occasions to perform in community music organizations. The high school student should be made aware of this wealth of musical activity.

The survey-of-music class in our school handles this task by maintaining a bulletin board of concert information and audition notices for community bands, orchestras, choruses, and musicals.

Information for the bulletin board is gleaned from newspaper advertisements, posters, university public relations releases, and radio announcements and is presented weekly in an attractive display showing each event's date, time, place, prices, and ticket sales locations. The bulletin board is located at the entrance to the music room and is clearly visible to all.

Students in our survey-of-music class gain experience in searching out local music events, while all students keep abreast of the city's musical scene.—*Janet F. Ban, Montour High School, McKees Rocks, Pennsylvania*

Resources Depend on Goals

In the past, students have either benefitted or suffered according to a teacher's strengths or weaknesses because, to a great extent, learning in the classroom has been controlled by the teacher. In recent years, music education programs have been severely affected by the difficulty in appealing to the more physically active and less motivated students. This has prompted music educators to alter traditional teaching techniques. One method that has become popular is for the teacher to make use of community resource persons for in-class instruction.

A positive atmosphere in which students can become more sensitized to the realities of music can be established by identifying and scheduling competent resource musicians to enter the classroom for educational purposes. Thus, a reciprocal benefit is experienced: the students profit from community people being in the classroom and the community becomes a more integral part of school activity. Such a program provides a broader range of options for students to experience music through history, theory, and performance. In addition, students learn how music is an essential part of our present-day environment and culture. These experiences can be a catalyst for discovery by infusing the students with a spirit of inquiry.

To structure and organize such a program, the teacher must first devise short- and long-range goals and behavioral objectives to determine the general focus of the program. Second, the teacher must become aware of community resource people by establishing contacts with parents and other key individuals in the area. Such contact can lead to resources such as rock musicians who attend the school, older amateur or professional musicians, relatives or friends of well-known musicians, or even retired music educators. Each resource can be put to use according to the goals and objectives of the teacher.—*Reginald T. Buckner, assistant professor of music education and Afro-American studies, University of Minnesota, Minneapolis*

Psychology + Social Work + Music

In the area of community resources, mental health professionals, both because of their academic knowledge of human behavior and their clinical skills for promoting growth and development, are of special value to educators. The specialties of psychology and social work seem to have the most potential for contributing to the school music program.

Psychologists and social workers are available to music educators from two realms: agencies and the school system's pupil personnel services. Community agencies, particularly those within publicly-financed community mental health programs, generally have, by statutory definition and governmental regulation, a commitment to provide other professionals with education and consultation that can facilitate mental health objectives; school personnel, such as music educators, would certainly be in the category of "other professionals."

A school system's pupil personnel services typically consist of psychologists, social workers, special educators for the disabled, and others. The school psychologist and the school social worker can, then, appropriately be recruited into the music program.

Perhaps the most basic area in which psychologists and social workers can be involved is in the administration and interpretation of tests for music interests and aptitudes. Two things should be noted. First, by nature of their training, psychologists have expertise in the use of standardized tests. Second, while many music educators might be capable of administering and scoring standardized music tests, psychologists and social workers can augment the technicalities with special knowledge of human behavior for the interpretation of the tests. Obviously, test scores mean essentially nothing without interpretation and translation into what the test scores suggest should be done vis-a-vis involvement with music within a behavioral context.

Individual behavior analysis is another area in which music education can be complemented by an integration with psychology and social work. It involves analyzing the conditions within a child's life to determine specific factors that reinforce the occurrence of certain behavioral acts. Such an understanding of what reinforces a child to respond in a particular way could allow the music educator to arrange positive conditions for motivating a child to learn music.

Similarly, group analysis can be used to determine interpersonal factors that influence a child's incentive to participate in music ensembles and to actively pursue learning music. Group analysis detects the connections, both positive and negative, between children, and can be used to understand why a child might be withdrawn or timid and thus be reserved in commitment to and motivation for involvement in music.

As with individual behavior analysis, group analysis can allow the educator to maximize learning conditions through understanding interpersonal reinforcement systems.

Behavior modification has proven to be especially applicable to music education. Psychologists and social workers with extensive academic preparation in behavior modification theory and techniques can serve as consultants to music educators and can help the educator previously unfamiliar with behavior modification to attain the adequate knowledge to make effective use of the reinforcement principles.

Self-explorations are critical to human development; all people should be introspective about needs and motives and should attempt to fit these into reality as a way of charting an acceptable path through life. Since this clearly falls into the psychological realm, it is apparent that special knowledge of human behavior would be helpful. In music education, self-exploration is important to a student's involvement in music study and performance. Through either one-on-one consultation or in-service training, psychologists and social workers can join with music educators to plan methods by which students can be helped to integrate music interests and aspirations into their life patterns.

Teacher consultation involves a psychologist or social worker serving in a "resource-peer" role for the music educator in helping to understand how to develop good interpersonal conditions within the music classroom. It should be recognized that the consultation relationship is one of equality, with the psychologist of social worker offering some specialized knowledge in an area unfamiliar to the educator while benefiting from consultation with a music educator if the objective under consideration is musical in nature.

Finally, the music educator can turn to a psychologist or social worker for information about the developmental characteristics of both normal and exceptional children. Human development does, indeed, involve stages that have unique characteristics that will influence a person's interest in and ability for music learning and performance.—*Robert Henley Woody, dean for graduate studies and research, professor of psychology, and lecturer in music, and Jane Divita Woody, assistant professor of social work, the University of Nebraska at Omaha*

And Don't Overlook...

When music educators turn their attention to community resources, it is often the case that the most immediate items are overlooked. Not enough attention is given to the parents of students, who in many cases may have a great deal to offer toward the enrichment of students' cultural and community understanding. In some communities, there may be parents who are first- or second-generation immigrants, and who may therefore be able to relate firsthand experiences in the music traditions and cultural idioms of their ethnic heritage. These experiences might include folk songs or dances, traditional festivals, or even instruments unique to a certain culture.

Another major resource that should be investigated is that of professional music companies: symphony orchestras, opera companies, and dance companies. Many of these are involved in various community-oriented activities that would be of interest in a general music education program. The Opera Company of Boston, for example, runs the Opera New England Program, which seeks to educate children in one of the less-familiar media of musical expression. The program offers in-school assemblies in communities throughout New England and, in addition, offers study guides for student operas. Professional music companies in other metropolitan areas are regularly becoming involved in similar programs.

At a national level, the Music Performance Trust Fund (MPTF), in conjunction with the American Federation of Musicians, sponsors performances and lectures in schools by nationally known musicians. This may be a once-in-a-lifetime chance for students to come into direct contact with famous musicians. Because MPTF acts as a sponsor, there may be no cost to the school, although cosponsorship is urged. If one of your chief goals for your class is to stimulate interest in the possibility of a career in music, such exposure to music professionals offers an excellent opportunity for this.

Of course, career education programs should not concentrate on performance aspects alone. A few minutes of thought, reference to the yellow pages of the telephone directory, or perhaps contact with local business organizations may lead to identifying a number of specialists who could be invited into the classroom to describe their work and answer questions—music publishers, disc jockeys, retailers, talent managers, composers, critics, music therapists, and so on.

Resources that are often overlooked are the community service organizations: the chamber of commerce, the department of recreation, arts councils, and so forth. These may be vast banks of information concerning upcoming events, performances, and festivals. If you post a list in your classroom of music activities in your community, then these organizations can be a good resource in keeping a list of this sort comprehensive and up-to-date.

An additional suggestion is to check with your public library about audiovisual products that they might be able to get for you. In recent years, many libraries have substantially improved the availability of recordings and films, and some libraries have sound studios for listening to recordings and equipment to preview films. Because of the aural and performance aspects of music, it seems to be a subject better suited to the augmentation of audiovisual programs than other areas of study, such as reading and mathematics.

Within any community, there are resources that the music educator can use to enliven the class and stimulate the interest of the students. Since music, music traditions, and musical tastes are different in every community, the music teacher should keep these resources in mind in trying to make his or her program as interesting and as relevant as possible.—*Peter B. Oliver, editorial assistant,* MEJ.

Music must be made available to as much of the adult population as possible, and this must be done in a way that builds an "intellectualized appreciation" of music. This does not mean that only the learned can enjoy music, but that the musically educated person can understand what he or she hears and performs, and enjoys it more than those who accept music blindly or with maudlin affection.

Expanding Music Education to all Segments of Society

by A. W. VanderMeer

While musicians have not always been honored, the art of music has been given prestige and recognition by the giants of Western thought and culture since the days of the Reformation. In fact, Martin Luther himself said, "Next to theology I give to music the highest place and honor." Thomas Morley set to music the words "When griping griefs the heart would wound, / and doleful dumps the mind oppress, / then music, with her silver sound / with speed is wont to send redress."

The seventeenth-century Restoration dramatist William Congreve implied that music makes other people easier to live with in what is perhaps the most commonly quoted passage about music: "Music has charmes to soothe the savage breast, to soften rocks, and bend the knotted oak." Congreve's sentiment is echoed and extended by Burritt: "Among the instrumentalities of love and peace, surely there can be no sweeter, softer, more effective voice than that of gentle, peace-breathing music."

If such sentiments as these have been expressed for several hundred years, and if they seem today to be thought of as eternal verities, why the present-day concern with expanding music education to all segments of society? We can seek answers in the changing nature of society that brings with it changing needs and changing priorities, or we can recall that the amount of time that elapses between the statement of a truth and its application is sometimes excessive. At the 1967 Tanglewood Symposium, philosopher Harry Broudy said:

> In urging more and better aesthetic education before this conference, not only am I preaching to the converted, but to the missionaries themselves. This too is worth doing, I suppose, in order to restore zeal that even among the faithful occasionally flags. However, a more important reason for seeking justification for aesthetic education is that if our cause if just, it is not obviously so (and certainly it is not obvious to those who provide the time and money for public schooling).[1]

In view of reports from the width and breadth of this land that the "fads" and "frills" of music and the purveyors thereof—music educators—are becoming casualties of the financial desperation of school districts, Broudy spoke more wisely than he knew.

If there is one message that is crystal clear in the expressions of philosophers regarding music, it is that there is an urgent and perennial necessity for making music available to as much of the

A. W. VanderMeer is a former professor and dean emeritus of the College of Education at the Pennsylvania State University. This article originally appeared in the December 1975 Music Educators Journal.

population as possible and that it should be made available in a way that will cultivate an intellectualized appreciation of, as distinguished from a blind acceptance of or a maudlin affection for, the art of music. Yet, there is clearly no place in the movement for the person who believes that only the learned, the profound, the complex, or the unintelligible is worthy of the name of music.

It may be useful to place all people—children, adolescents, and adults—in three categories according to the way they relate to music—users, citizens, and performers. Obviously, these are not mutually exclusive categories since any person can, at different times, be found in any of these categories. We can then establish a hierarchy of behavioral characteristics and set progress up the hierarchy as a goal for each individual.

Users
- They like some kind of music.
- They like several kinds of music.
- They obtain music for their own use by, at the very least, tuning it in on the radio and by, at best, buying it and furnishing their homes with means for reproducing it.
- They discriminate in their liking according to some standard.
- They know why they discriminate.
- There is some agreement between their discrimination and that of cultivated taste as expressed by "experts."

Citizens
- They advocate (support the cause of, react favorably to, reinforce) music activities within their families.
- They advocate music among their friends.
- They advocate music in their communities, including the schools and other institutions.
- They advocate the support of music at the national level.

Performers
- They sing or whistle.
- They join in—such as in church or in singing the national anthem.

- They join an organized group.
- They study to improve their performances.
- They rent or buy an instrument.
- They develop their performance skills.

Obviously, these are not all the behavioral characteristics that could be cited. It must also be understood that these objectives are dynamic ones and that the achievement of them is progressive. The aim, in general, is to move the largest possible portion of the population toward the higher end of each of the three continuums.

Points of Entry
The largest groups of people who can take an active part in achieving the objective of extending music to the widest segment of our society are, of course, the teachers of music and their able allies, the music supervisors. These groups generally work in two settings: the school and the community. Little needs to be said about the school setting because most professional music educators have a clear understanding of the relationship between the goals of the general music curriculum and the goals of a broad expansion of music to the rest of society. However, it may be worthwhile to restate a few basic concepts pertinent to the school setting.

It is generally agreed that good music teachers possess the following characteristics: they know the key concepts, modes of inquiry, standards of evidence, and problems to be solved in the field of music; their music skills are developed enough to be effective in demonstrating and explaining; and they are familiar with enough music literature to be able to prescribe appropriate works for each individual learner. They should also be able to distinguish and prescribe adequately for the achievement of goals in the cognitive, the affective, and the psychomotor domains. These domains cannot be treated separately, and it is entirely possible that too much concentration on one may hinder achievement in the others. Thus, the common error of attempting to reach the affective domain (liking or appreciating music) by way of the cognitive domain (recognizing and understanding structures of music) is generally avoided.

If a music educator is to succeed in expanding music to the broader society, he or she must locate the available points of entry. Obviously, the most accessible point of entry is the school. Few professional groups have as great an opportunity to influence from within the school what goes on outside the formal classroom and, indeed, what spills over into the community, as do the music teachers and the music supervisors. However, this influence is not always positive. The need for producing performance groups that will draw favorable comments from important critics is often in direct conflict with the objectives of expanding music to wider segments of the population. Music teachers, like all professionals, need to be appreciated, and this appreciation comes all too often through excellence in performing groups. Music teachers rarely advance in salary and rank because they have widened the horizons of music for the relatively uncultured segments of the population; rather, they advance because they have produced outstanding performance groups. Hard choices often must be made, since resources of time and energy are almost always limited. My hat is off to the educator who chooses in favor of general music and of working in the school and community with the less-experienced performance groups.

Know Your Target Audiences

In a society that places high value on equal opportunity and on the thought of all people being created equal, it is distasteful to recognize that it *does* matter who you are and that, since that matters, it also matters whom you approach and whose support you seek in activities designed to bring music to all segments of society. Anyone who hopes to gain support for music must identify the people or groups in his or her community that fit in the following four categories: those that are powers in the community and are pro-music, those that are powers in the community and are anti-music, those that are not influential in the community and are pro-music, and those that are

not influential in the community and are anti-music. Obviously, the support of those in the first category should be sought first. They are the ones who can convert those in the second category—if anyone can—and both of those groups can then bring along those in the last two categories.

The media are another important point of entry into the larger community. Surveys have shown that most children spend as much, if not more, time with the mass media—especially radio and television—as they do with schools, and a large portion of this time is devoted exclusively to music or to listening and viewing that is accompanied by music. Therefore, a music educator must be concerned with the media because they can support or contradict his or her own aims. There are three lines of attack: The first is the obvious one of using the media in formal and informal educational settings. The music teacher needs to know what students and other members of the community are listening to. Knowing this, of course, is hardly enough; some intervention is also required. Reference to current themes of the cinema and television, to rated tunes, to current performers, and so on are vital in formal music classes. A music educator can actually get involved with the media by writing columns for the local papers, working for the local radio or television station as a music critic, or writing letters to the editor.

In the broader national field, the music educator can try to bring about changes for the betterment of music. For example, it seems completely incongruous that a four- or five-hundred-dollar television set comes equipped with the same four- or five-inch side-mounted speaker as does the cheapest portable radio. Television manufacturers are in the business of making money, and informed and vigorous protest might make a difference. By the same token, the influence of music educators can be felt on the programming of local radio stations, or the programming of artists' series, on the quality of music accompaniment of television shows and other presentations, and so on.

Acting in the Public Interest

Third, the music educator has an obligation to do what he or she can, as a citizen, to influence the media to act in the public interest. The best of music on television in wonderful; the worst is terrible. The tragedy is that the worst occupies several hundred more broadcast hours per week than does the best. At an MENC meeting in Atlanta, an apologist for a major network blamed the low quality of a music program for schools on the reluctance of the network to invest $300,000 in revising and correcting the videotapes. That seems like quite a large amount until one considers what a college football team is paid for a major bowl appearance. Of course, a network is a profit-making organization, but it does not *own* the airways; it is granted the use of them by an instrumentality of the government and is expected to use them *in the public interest*. If music educators don't wish to make noises about how the public interest is served in the elevation of music tastes, they can support public broadcasting. Both approaches are recommended.

I strongly support one of MENC's formally stated aims: to broaden and enhance the music literacy and taste of the entire population of this country.

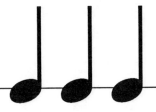

Section

Opportunities for Music Educators

What are some ways that music educators can reach everyone in their communities, including adults and senior citizens? In this section, closed by an article by Charles Elliott on singing in America, several authors describe their successful programs.

Adult education often includes musical activities but does not always offer adults the opportunity to study music as beginners. Music educators must be flexible enough to deal with beginners of all ages and to make the adjustments needed to accommodate adult needs, wishes, schedules, and other aspects that are different from those of younger students.

Adult Beginners:
Music Education's New Frontier

by Donald W. Forrester

From the young executive taking evening courses to complete a once-forsaken degree program, the middle-aged matron studying French to make her trip abroad more meaningful, to the young homemaker enrolled in business course, we have become a national of college drop-ins. Though we are not as concerned about degrees as we once were, we are demonstrating increased interest in learning for self-improvement, both for the personal satisfaction of gaining new knowledge and for the unabashed fun of it.

This search for knowledge is by no means limited to the traditional academic disciplines. Recently, a local newspaper carried a feature story about a college professor who had just completed a course in bricklaying at a nearby technical and vocational school. A large university in a nearby city frequently advertises noncredit courses in everything from bridge to parapsychology, as well as in some of the more traditional subjects, including art and music.

Donald W. Forrester is the director of Continued Education in Teaching and Learning (CETL) and teaches in the music department at Kennesaw State College, PO Box 444, Marietta, GA 30061. When this article was published, he was head of the music department at Georgia Southwestern College, Americus. This article originally appeared in the December 1975 Music Educators Journal.

Continuing Education in Music

We need to examine carefully the ways in which music can be included in adult education programs. Many of us in the teaching profession are frequently heard to express some interest in helping members of our communities learn about music, but all we do is sit them down in front of our performance groups and bombard their ears with whatever it is we have decided they should hear. Our intentions may be beyond criticism, but the results, unhappily, fall short of our expectations. We may temporarily soothe our guilt for having failed to meet the musical needs of such a large segment of society, but most of us never pursue the problem any further.

Adult education, or continuing education if you prefer, offers us valuable opportunities for involving the public more actively with music. Of course, this suggestion is not new. Fine programs already exist at large universities and at some of the smaller community colleges. However, interested music educators can give more attention to this area than they are now doing. Wherever an adult evening program is being operated without regular offerings in music, those of us interested in working with adults are likely to find a receptive atmosphere, but is the public really interested? An adequate number of students enroll in order to justify the offering of a new course. However, the fact that both state and private colleges continue to offer music courses quarter after quarter seems to indicate at least some support.

As the head of a small music department in a community college, I have been receiving an increasing number of request for music instruction in addition to that offered as part of our regular academic program. In recent months, several fellow civic club members have asked, with studied casualness, "Is there anyone at the college who could teach me to play the guitar (or piano)?" Other people in town frequently call to ask if voice lessons are available for nonstudents. A local elementary school principal expressed interest in singing in a chorus and wondered if the college might sponsor a group for adults in the community. Perhaps the most interesting request came from a young minister who promised to supply ten class members (the minimum number for one of our adult evening courses) if the college would offer a group piano course. It seems that his Sunday-school pianists needed to improve their playing. The college has an eighteen-unit electronic piano studio that is never used after 5:00 P.M., so why not? Indeed, the response to all these requests is "why not?"

The First Rungs of the Ladder

One reason why not is the apparent unwillingness on the part of many academic musicians to descend from their pedestals long enough to meet people where their *present* music interests lie. Somehow it seems intellectually disreputable to teach a group of adults to play simple music on a guitar or a piano. Why? Must all music be esoteric, even for the fledgling who wants to include music in his or her life but lacks the aesthetic and technical resources to do so? Let's be honest. Wasn't there a time when all of us enjoyed simple, basic music? We may have forgotten and we have doubtless outgrown some once-valuable experiences with music, but all of us began by enjoying a kind of music that seems only in retrospect to have been technically undemanding. Adult beginners have to start in much the same way, and not all college-level instructors are willing or even able to provide this kind of guidance. Thus, this teaching must be done by a person with special qualities.

A second deterrent to adult music instruction is the ill-founded but widely accepted belief that adults can no longer develop the psychomotor skills necessary to play an instrument. This belief belongs in the same wastebasket with the idea that the adult mind can no longer function effectively in absorbing new information. Both beliefs disregard human individuality. Highly motivated adults of all ages take up painting, earn degrees, and master any of a number of skills usually thought of as being in the domain of the young. It is probably true that an adult beginner should not expect to become a great instrumentalist, but I have seen some who have become competent performers, able to play for their own enjoyment and for the pleasure of others.

Sharing the Workload

One objection often voiced by the potential instructors of adult courses is that they are usually held, of necessity, at night. Few teachers relish the idea of being taken away from home and social and cultural activities several nights a week, especially if they teach during the day as well. While the problem is a real one, part of it can be solved administratively. A professor teaching afternoon and evening courses could be assigned no morning classes, and he or she could be excused from morning office hours. Some individuals work best at night and would prefer to do so. In the case where faculty members are not to be found, an administrator could rotate evening teaching assignments.

Unfortunately, the evening programs at many colleges have a second-class image, fostered by the attitude that since many of the courses are noncredit, the most qualified faculty members need not be employed. Salaries for teaching these courses are often considerably less than for daytime courses, even when highly qualified teachers are available. Sometimes a person who teaches full-time during the day will teach an evening course to supplement his or her income, taking a highly reduced rate of pay. Such a situation presents two problems: First, there is a limit to how far a person can stretch his or her effectiveness; second, it makes no sense for a teacher to receive less compensation for extra hours spent practicing his or her profession. The ideal, of course, would be to secure highly qualified people who prefer to teach full-time in the evening program, and to provide remuneration commensurate with that of others of similar academic rank.

The Benefits of Teaching Adults

Though there are disadvantages, to be sure, there are also enormous attractions to teaching adults. First, consider who these learners are—leaders in the community, executives, homemakers and professional people, mechanics and public servants—your contemporaries, neighbors, and colleagues. Next, consider why they are there. It is not for the purpose of learning a salable skill nor for the prestige of earning a degree. Certainly they are not there because of parental or peer-group pressure. They are there simply because they want to learn something they believe to be valuable—perhaps the purest of all motives for learning. Individuals with a large amount of motivation bring to the learning situation a contagious kind of enthusiasm that is often missing from the average classroom. Finally, consider the reward of seeing interested, inquisitive people

achieving a sense of aesthetic fulfillment and establishing a foundation on which to continue their interest in music throughout the remainder of their lifetimes.

In addition to all of this, there is a bonus. People who involve themselves personally in the arts seem to become more interested in the artistic contributions of others. Isn't it true that virtually every noncommercial music enterprise in the country needs greater public support? Professional and civic symphonies need monetary support; college music departments need scholarship money in order to encourage young performers; and school systems need public support in providing high-quality music programs for our nation's children. Besides financial and moral support, people themselves are needed, for music without listeners is an unfulfilled art.

Our profession is committed to providing quality music education, and our willingness to fulfill this commitment should not be influenced by the age of the learner. Not all teachers can or should teach adult beginners. At a time of rapid and radical change in the profile of higher education, however, when indications are that continuing education will become a larger part of the colleges' business, music education needs to change, too, and prepare to venture into a new frontier.

The Arizona State University West Campus confronted the question of how to attract its predominantly adult students to the fine arts. Arts events were scheduled on the basis of criteria related to the specific audience the arts educators wanted to attract, as were the objectives of arts courses. The "Arts Awareness" courses combine fun, learning, and social involvement. They also increase students' perceptive skills in the arts.

An Arts Program for Adults

by Elayne Achilles

How does a new branch campus attract its student population of mostly adult learners to the fine arts? Curriculum planners confronted this question when developing the course offerings for a new extension of Arizona State University in Phoenix, known as the ASU West Campus.

When it was suggested that an audience awareness course be offered in music, faculty members in all the fine arts programs wanted to participate. As a result, an interdisciplinary fine arts undergraduate elective, titled "Arts Awareness," was developed. As originally envisioned, the course was to consist of a series of lectures given before performers of local music events so that concertgoers might become better listeners. In its expanded form, the course included attendance at eight performances and exhibits in art, dance, music, and drama. Lectures were presented by members of the fine arts faculty in conjunction with visiting artists and lecturers.

The Students

What kind of student would be attracted to this type of course? The catalog description said the course was "designed for members of the community and non-arts majors interested in increasing

Elayne Achilles is an assistant professor of fine arts at Arizona State University West Campus, Phoenix. This article originally appeared in the April 1988 issue of the Music Educators Journal.

perceptive skills in the arts." Respondents included a retired woman who teaches international folk dance at a local adult community center, a winter visitor interested in the culture of the area, a children's librarian in charge of education services at the public library, a medical doctor who sings in his church choir, a high school dance teacher, and a commercial photographer completing a liberal arts degree. Most of the students audited the course since they wanted the experience, not the credit. The variety of interests, needs, and abilities of this diverse population was bewildering at first. Class discussions, however, revealed a richness of experience that seemed to deepen mutual respect and cohesiveness.

Arts Events

Selecting the events on which to base the course was not easy. The four lecturers, one each in the areas of art, dance, drama, and music, met with the coordinator, and all shared the current roster of events in each art medium. Two events were scheduled in each area with a lecture before and after the event whenever possible. It was agreed that a lecture and discussion after each event was important for immediate feedback, as was a preparatory lecture. Criteria for selecting events were (a) appropriateness of the event for a novice, (b) convenience in scheduling with other events and lectures, (c) reasonable ticket prices, and (d) the lecturer's familiarity with the event. After the frustration of initial scheduling, arrangements were made with less difficulty than anticipated. When one theater director was contacted about ordering block tickets for a play, he invited the class to a private lecture at the theater before the preview performance and the entire class was admitted at no charge. In a similar manner, other arts centers provided half-price tickets, an added bonus for the students. By tapping into university-sponsored programs, some concerts were free. The class also had the privilege of a private viewing of the art lecturer's sculpture exhibit at a local gallery, which stayed open after hours just for the class.

Course Objectives

What did the students learn from the course? The long-range goals for the students were to:

- increase their perceptive, analytical skills in the arts,
- enhance their personal aesthetic awareness of the arts,
- experience art concepts from the artist's perspective, and
- increase their motivation, knowledge, and skills sufficiently so that these would enhance personal and active participation in one or more of the arts.

The instructors established the following specific objectives for the class, stating that the participants, at the end of the semester of study, should be able to:

- describe how each art form conveys meaning,
- describe the main elements of style in each art medium,
- summarize the content of performances and exhibits of arts events,
- compare stylistic elements among various art media, and
- compare the artist's perspective to personal perspectives.

These objectives focus on helping the interested beginner think like an artist. To think like an artist, one needs to be familiar with the descriptive vocabulary of each medium. Lecturers—artists themselves—talked about concepts such as the "felt space" between a sculpture and the viewer, about the

editing liberties a director must assume in producing a play, or about the difference between "referential" and "abstract" forms in dance, music, or the visual arts.

Evaluation

To help organize their experiences, students wrote reaction papers after each event. Guidelines for the papers included these topics and questions.

1. *Description:* Characterize what you saw or heard, using as many terms from the lecturer's vocabulary as possible.

2. *Style:* What is the style (or period) of this performance or exhibit? How does it vary from other styles within this art medium?

3. *Comparison:* Are there any contrasts or similarities between this event and other art media studied in class or from your personal experience?

4. *Personal viewpoint:* How does your view of this performance or exhibit compare with the artist's view? Are your views changing? Why or why not?

These guidelines reflected the course objectives. Lecturers agreed that, based on what they read in the reaction papers, the students seemed to be achieving the course goals. Students were also purchasing recordings of musical performances, attending events in addition to class offerings, and bringing guests to performances, all indications that the students were meeting these goals. The synthesis of experience and reflection was interesting to all participants. One student was visibly fearful of a particular sculpture that placed observers in a vulnerable position, kneeling at an altar while artificial lightning flashed from the ceiling. The student's reaction paper dealt with her fears, and the process of writing made her more aware of the powerful feelings the artist evoked.

Students were encouraged to submit course evaluations and suggestions for improvement. Their ideas included increasing the course from two to three credits, because members believed that more time for discussion of reactions to each event was needed. (The richness of the lecturer's knowledge, in addition to the experience of the events themselves, produced a flood of visual images, sounds, and ideas that was not easy to absorb in a short time.) Other suggestions involved the assignment of an essay to synthesize ideas from all the arts (a summary of the thoughts evoked in reaction papers) and the addition of topical readings to better prepare students for lectures.

One student recommended increased coordination of the content among the interdisciplinary staff so that all team members would be fully aware of the material being taught by their colleagues. This is especially difficult, since the course is partly taught by nonresident faculty. One solution might be to conduct a planning workshop to coordinate course content and improve the teaching skills of the staff and to use the resources of the university's faculty development program, which frequently offers grants for this type of staff improvement.

The possibilities for the future are exciting. One woman in the class took her husband to all the events, and he is planning to enroll in the next course and take her to all the events. Students quickly became friends in the informal social environment of the arts events. These interactions carried over to the more formal classroom lectures, making them appeal especially to the adult learner. Some of these students had not been in a university classroom for years and retained memories of past university experiences that were sometimes negative. The supportive, positive environment of the class made "going back again" a pleasant educational experience.

A course like "Arts Awareness" that combines fun, learning, and social involvement while increasing perceptive skills in the arts has a high probability of success.

The number of older Americans is rising rapidly, and educators have recognized the need of this population for education and the arts. The special requirements of older Americans should be assessed systematically when planning music and dance programs for them. Music programs should be comprehensive, and a wide variety of activities should be offered to accommodate more individuals with differing interests and abilities. Suggestions are made for arts instruction for older Americans, and Jessica Davidson describes her Maryland study of arts education for the elderly.

Music and Gerontology: A Young Endeavor

by Jessica B. Davidson

According to the United States Bureau of the Census, the number of Americans who are sixty-five years of age and over represents nearly 11 percent of the total population and is projected to rise to 13 percent—approximately 32 million individuals—by the year 2000. A growing number of older adults are participating in music programs in their communities, places of worship, civic organizations, continuing education classes, and various residential institutions for the aged. Many colleges and universities are making courses of instruction in their standard music and dance programs available without cost to older adults.

These programs of music and dance for older adults are providing a new vehicle for the skills and interests of music educators, but few broad-based efforts have been made to systematically assess the special needs of older Americans. Although much further research and analysis needs to be undertaken, some general recommendations can be made on the basis of a recent survey of the

Jessica B. Davidson formerly taught music in the Department of Aging at the University of Kentucky, Lexington. This article originally appeared in the May 1980 Music Educators Journal.

music programs at residential and nursing homes for the aged in Maryland.[1]

Curriculum

First and foremost, a program of music for older adults should be comprehensive. The more activities that are provided, the more individuals with differing interests and abilities will become actively involved. The older adult population includes both lovers of classical music and fans of the Top 40 singles.

A complete music curriculum for older adults should include the teaching of basic music reading and theory, preferably by the use of enlarged notes and staff. For instrumentalists, fingering, blowing, breath control, and other basic techniques are essential and should be adjusted to the level of the various students. Basic vocal instruction should be available, covering breath control, diction, placement, interpretation, and skills in both unison and part singing.

A simple choral curriculum could start with basic unison songs and progress to uncomplicated part work. If a group has a background in part work, a more extensive repertoire may be developed. Initially, folk songs, selections from musicals, religious literature, and popular songs of the twenties, thirties, forties, and fifties are likely to be of interest. From this point, a program could be expanded according to the capabilities of the participants. Songfests and sing-alongs are excellent ways to involve a large number of individuals. The recruitment of a good pianist, drummer, and bass or guitar player to accompany singing activities can add further enthusiasm to large-group singing.

Class dance instruction should begin with basic steps and progress through more advanced social and ethnic types of dance. Dance programs provide a welcome social outlet for many older adults and, in addition, involve them in needed physical activity. Again, instruction must accommodate the various ability levels of the participants.

Adaptations must be made for the physical, mental, and social problems of the elderly both in and out of institutions. Small wooden music racks that can be placed on tables are excellent. A lap board that attached to the sides of a wheelchair is useful for holding music books. Lap boards are also helpful for bed patients who can sit up. Instruments can be secured to the sides of a wheelchair or bed, and music can be focused on the ceiling with an overhead projector for patients who must remain prone. Transparencies should be made with enlarged staves, notes, and words.

A small music library should be included in centers, clubs, institutions, and community settings serving the elderly. Books, magazines, and journals pertaining to all phases of music and other arts are essential. A complete library should include substantial audiovisual equipment—sound equipment, film and filmstrip projectors, audiocassettes, disc recordings, videotapes, and films. Such a library can serve as the basis for a music listening program.

Keys to Success

While studying music programs for the elderly in Maryland, I found several common underlying features of successful music programs for older Americans. Dedicated, enthusiastic leadership is of great importance. Programs organized and directed by music teachers, retired professional musicians, or staff or community volunteers with music backgrounds seem to be more efficiently planned and capable of maintaining greater participation than programs developed by nonmusicians.

Recruitment of qualified leaders can be undertaken through careful advertising and publicity and through contacts with national, state, and local music organizations. Retired music teachers often prove to be fine program leaders; their age level and experience contribute to an empathetic approach, and they are included to recognize and exhibit consideration for the physiological, psychological, and sociological factors involved in working with elderly persons.

The success of a music program is also in direct ratio to the adequacy of equipment and materials. In institutions where large-print songbooks, choral music, and instrumental books are provided, programs can be more extensive. Facilities that supplied a variety of instruments, tapes, disc recordings, reading materials, and sound equipment were consistently rated by respondents in the Maryland study as offering music programs of superior quality. A publicity campaign can produce public donations of instruments, books, materials, equipment, and publications. Civic and community organizations can be persuaded to provide transportation to musical events and to reduce ticket costs for senior citizens.

My study of Maryland programs also indicated that the institutions for the elderly that are church-affiliated or members of a commercial chain generally offer more comprehensive music or dance programs. In many instances, a program coordinator supervises all the arts programs within a chain of homes. Individual institutions within chains also usually provide a recreation or program director. In Maryland, community colleges that belong to the Maryland Consortium of Gerontology Departments offer a variety of music courses for older adults, frequently taught within institutions or senior citizen centers. Where such academic participation exists, the quality of the overall music program is usually superior.

Another key to the success of a music program for older adults is the general attitude toward the program of administrators, owners, recreation and social directors, service directors, and all other staff members. A negative or apathetic atmosphere can limit or destroy a music program. Some respondents in my study suggested that a short in-service course should be offered in nearby colleges or universities to train program directors for implementing successful music programs in their institutions or community centers.

The success of music programs also depends on accurately defining and assessing the capabilities of the participants. All too often the full range of their talents remains unrecognized and untapped. Even ninety-year-olds are frequently capable of much more than merely singing. I also found that instrumental programs, when adequately funded, staffed, and equipped, are well-attended and successful. Such programs require regular scheduling and a progressive course of study. Bell choirs, small wind ensembles, and classes in recorder, guitar, Autoharp, and percussion can be popular. In some institutions and centers musicals can be produced, as can dance reviews and dance band programs.

Administrators of music programs for older adults should not overlook or slight the social element of music and dance activities. Many otherwise uninterested persons enjoy attending parties, holiday dances, and trips to outside social events that involve music. Many older individuals feel deeply lonely. Institutions often try to combat this feeling by offering social events that encourage residents to mingle and make friends. The value of such occasions does not lie in their musical worth alone.

Starting a Program

The establishment of a music program for older adults should be preceded by careful research. Try to visit senior centers, golden-age clubs, retirement complexes and villages, and institutions for the elderly in nearby areas, and study the different music programs they offer. Visit departments of gerontology in area colleges and universities to study their library materials on aging. An extensive library at the National Council on the Aging contains much helpful material. The American Medical Association publishes books that address the sociological, physiological, and psychological aspects of aging. Other organizations and agencies that can supply helpful information include the American Association of Retired Persons, the National Citizens Coalition for Nursing Home Reform, and state departments on aging. Do not overlook the sources of potential help in your own community: schools, places of worship, civic organizations, and clubs.

Planners also should conduct an inventory of equipment and materials available and also consider the staff necessary to sustain the program. A music therapist may be an asset in a program that includes physically disabled participants. It would be advantageous if all staffers to be involved in a music program would take a semester-long course as minimal training for working with older adults. Many universities currently provide courses in music for special education; doubtless some will soon be adding courses in music for elderly adults.

A survey of the population to be served should be conducted to define the areas of their interest in music. A general set of plans for each type of music activity should provide a framework on which to build. The initial schedule of classes and music activities should be publicized extensively.

Materials

Only a limited amount of music is published specifically for older adults at present, but several companies publish materials adaptable to the elderly, particularly sheet music and collections with large notes and staves.

Mel Bay Publications offers beginning guitar books, recorder beginner editions, and dulcimer books with enlarged notes. The Mel Bay *Fun Series* includes folk song collections and books for accordion, alto recorder, Autoharp, banjo, baritone, ukulele, drums, dulcimer, electric bass, harmonica, guitar, jaw harp, mandolin, tenor banjo, piano, and organ. Mel Bay also publishes a piano book titled *Easy-Way Play* that uses a simple chord method adaptable for older keyboard beginners.

Shawnee Press publishes choral books of interest to older adults: *Rock around the 50's* for three-part treble voices, *A Choral Portrait* of Irving Berlin songs, and *Twentiana* for SATB, SSAA, and TTBB, with optional bass and drums.

Willis Music Company publishes seventy big-note piano solos (grades I, I½, II) in the keys of C, F, G, and D major and G minor. According to the titles, twenty-eight of these would be of interest to older adults. Willis also carries Jenswold's *My Hymns* (simplified piano edition with words), Rosemond's *The Art of Music for the Adult Beginner* (piano), *At Christmastide*, and *Sing Together at Christmas* (piano with chord symbols and sing-along sheets). It also offers thirty-five piano solos listed specifically for older beginners. Seven of them have titles that should be familiar to the senior citizen.

The Boston Music Company publishes *Big Note Christmas Carols* and *Big Note Christmas Favorites* for piano. Boston also carries *Hymns for You To Play and Sing*, *Christmas Carols and Songs*, *The Rodgers and Hammerstein Recorder Book* (recorder and piano), *The Sound of Music* (handbell choir), *Christmas for Autoharp*, *Twenty-One Folk Songs for Autoharp*, *The Family Guitar Book*, *A Day at a Time* (guitar chords), *How To Play the Dulcimer*, *Meet the Harmonica*, *Pocket-Mate Mandolin Chords*, *The Musical Bingo Game*, *Rodgers and Hammerstein for C and G Portable Chord Organ*, *Easy-To-Play Piano Collections*, and *Rodgers and Hammerstein Singtime* (arranged for unison voices with optional voice).

The Neil A. Kjos Company publishes the *Bastien Older Beginner Piano Library* for levels I and II with supplementary materials, including *Classic Themes by the Masters*, *Religious Favorites*, and *Easy Piano Classics*. . The series includes theory, technique, and sight-reading materials. Kjos also carries the *Bastien Older Beginner Organ Library*, a four-phase course designed for students from twelve to eighty, with a method book, a musicianship edition, and a pedal-skills book for levels I and II. Collections include *Great Christmas Carols*, *Great Classic Themes*, and *Great Hymns*. This company also publishes *A Guide for Piano Instruction for the Educationally Blind*, a course of study designed to adapt beginning piano books for blind students.

Hal Leonard Publishing offers a substantial line of large-note/large-staff editions in their *E-Z Play Today* series for organ, piano, and guitar. This series offers *E-Z Play Today Piano Sing-along Standards*, *E-Z Play Today Piano Beginnings*, and *E-Z Play Today Jumbo Songbook*. Several items from their 114 listings could be of use with older adults, such as *Beginnings*, *Dance Band Giants*, *Hits from Musicals*, *Patriotic Songs*, *Christmas Time*, *All Time Requests*, *Celebrated Favorites*, *Country Pickin's*, *Fireside Singalong*, and *Sing Along Standards*. Others include *Sacred Sounds*, *Memorable Standards*, *Sentimental Ballads*, *Songs of the 20s*, *Songs of the 30s*, *Nostalgic Tunes*, *Sing Along Requests*, *Gospel Favorites*, *Christmas Songs*, *Favorite Hymns*, *It's Gospel*, *Gospel Greats*, *Hymns of Glory*, *Sacred Moments*, and *Movie Songs of the 30s and 40s*. Hal Leonard also publishes *Solos for Organs* in the *Solo Today* series, a step-by-step method with slightly enlarged notation. Another publication adaptable to older musicians is *The Sound of Christmas for Instant Orchestra*, designed for organ, piano, guitar, accordion and certain other instruments as a play-along activity. A cassette version is also available for play-along use. The *Solo Today* series includes *Inspirational Hymns* and *Top Requests*, published with enlarged notes.

The Library of Congress' National Library Service for the Blind and Physically Handicapped distributes occasional materials about music and musicians in Braille editions and disc recordings that may be useful for blind and other physically disabled older adults.

Looking Toward the Future

This listing is not all-inclusive. Program planners should write to other publishers in search of additional suitable music and materials.

Music educators of the near and far future must of necessity begin to consider where and how they can become involved in developing music experiences for older adults. The stage needs to be set before the curtain rises. What we have accomplished to date is not enough, but one possible route for the survival of our profession is to ensure that music programs for the older adult attain the status of a top priority by the year 2000.

Note

1. Jessica B. Davidson, "The Status of Music Programs for Residents of Sheltered Housing, Nursing and Domiciliary Care Homes in Maryland" (Ph.D. diss., University of Maryland, 1978).

Addresses of publishers and organizations mentioned in this article

American Association of Retired Persons
601 E Street NW
Washington, DC   20049
202-434-2277

American Medical Association
515 North Street
Chicago, IL   60610
312-464-5000

Mel Bay Publications, Inc.
4 Industrial Drive
Pacific, MO   63069
314-257-3970

Boston Music Company
172 Tremont Street
Boston, MA   02111
617-426-5100

Neil A. Kjos Music Company
4382 Jutland Drive
San Diego, CA   92117-0894
619-483-0501

Hal Leonard Publishing Corporation
7777 West Bluemound Road
Milwaukee, WI   53213
414-774-3630

Humanities and Prime Time
National Council on the Aging
409 Third Street SW, Suite 200
Washington, DC   20024
202-479-1200

National Citizens Coalition for
   Nursing Home Reform
1224 M Street NW, Suite 301
Washington, DC   20005
202-393-2018

National Library Service for the Blind
   and Physically Handicapped
Library of Congress
1291 Taylor Street NW
Washington, DC   20542
202-707-5100

Shawnee Press, Inc.
49 Waring Drive
Delaware Water Gap, PA   18327
717-476-0550

Willis Music Company
7380 Industrial Road
Florence, KY   41042
606-283-2050

The older population of the United States is increasing in number, and the elderly are becoming emancipated. They are no longer apathetic, and music plays an important role in the change of the older generation. Jessica B. Davidson describes the excellent program of the Council on Aging of the Department of University Extension, University of Kentucky, which brings active arts experiences to older Americans in Lexington and surrounding communities.

Music for the Young at Heart

by Jessica B. Davidson

Our older population is rapidly increasing at a surprising rate. In 1990, one of every five individuals were over fifty-five years of age. This segment of our population can be designated the senior-young since their attitudes and extensive activities, both social and academic, are prolonging interests, vocations, and hobbies of earlier periods in their lives: The stereotype of the rocking chair and the grandmother wrapped in a shawl is no longer accurate. Adults of the fifty, sixty, seventy, eighty, and even ninety age brackets are enjoying diversified activities ranging from belly dancing to intense academic study for advanced degrees.

Grandpa and Grandma are no longer chained to the television set. They represent an emancipated generation, alive and alert. The tarnish of apathy has been removed from the golden years, and they glisten with pleasure and fulfillment. Music is represented well in this renaissance of interests.

Program Overview

The Council on Aging of the Department of University Extension, University of Kentucky, Lexington, offers a diversified program of musical activities and courses for adults fifty years of age and over. Students are from Lexington and sur-

Jessica B. Davidson is the former director of music education, Council on Aging, University of Kentucky, Lexington. This article originally appeared in the May 1980 Music Educators Journal.

rounding communities and commute from as far as fifty miles. The median age of participants is approximately seventy-two. The primary goal of this program is active participation with music for senior adults.

Initially, contacts were made with organizations in Lexington and surrounding communities. Speeches about the program were given to civic groups such as Kiwanis, Shrine, and Lions; to senior centers; to clubs for older adults in churches such as Golden Years Clubs; and to senior-adult Sunday-school classes, community service organizations, and in high-rise apartment complexes housing senior adults.

The University of Kentucky's Council on Aging offers a scholarship program for adults ages sixty-five and over. The location of any program for the senior adult is of utmost importance. If free parking or bus accessibility is not available, some members of the program find it difficult to attend. Anyone considering implementation of an area music program for senior adults should be aware of the problems involved with transportation to and from the site. Classes are held two days a week, and individual classes meet once a week. In addition to the courses offered in the fall semester, two sections of Rudiments of Music are offered for the spring semester. This replaces a music appreciation course.

A jazz ensemble is an outgrowth of the orchestra and plays music of the 1930s, '40s, and '50s. It performs for civic organizations and clubs in the area. Rehearsals are held on weekends and have evolved into special gatherings, as well. The social impact on all groups in the area music program is great.

Course Offerings

All performance groups present Christmas and spring concerts. In 1980, the orchestra prepared works including the Alfred Burt carols, yuletide selections, and a festival arrangement of "White Christmas" performed with the mixed chorus. That year, the mixed chorus prepared an extensive program of selections from Bach to contemporary Christmas music. Students of the four instruments offered for lessons played traditional carols for the Christmas program. The previous year, the orchestra and chorus presented the *Nutcracker Suite* and a cantata as joint offerings. At the present time, the orchestra, mixed chorus, and instrumental students are preparing ambitious arrangements of music from three Broadway musicals for their spring concert.

Instruction books used for beginner's basic study are listed at the end of this article. This is not an exclusive list, but is included as a possible guide for instructors implementing new programs with senior adults.

Music of the twenties, thirties, forties, and fifties, taught during the fall semester, includes familiar popular and folk songs, instrumental and vocal recordings of a variety of musical selections, and discussions of twentieth-century composers' lives and works. Recordings used for the popular folk songs and band selections are taken from two collections procured through the *Reader's Digest* titled *The Golden Age of Entertainment* (113 selections) and *Mood Music for Dining* (129 selections). These collections include ten records each and feature music of varied types, including copies of many famous band and vocal recordings of the four decades, as well as classical selections. Program notes are included with dates of the compositions as well as information about the composers and a brief history of each work. Recordings of the music of twentieth-century composers are procured from libraries.

Many handout materials are used for these classes. Where typing is involved, triple spacing and the use of all capital letters were found to facilitate reading for students who have vision problems. Part of each class period is spent singing songs of the decade being studied, another for listening to band and vocal recordings, and another for a discussion of the twentieth-century composers and listening to their recordings. The latter segment was found to require much more time, and adjustments were frequently made to accommodate the discussions and recordings of twentieth-century composers' works.

The Rudiments of Music encompasses basic theory and is a useful course to offer. The course covers the treble and bass staves; major and minor scales; intervals, inversions, and alterations; triads; chords (major and minor keys); inversions of chords with figured bass and simple four-part writing; transposition; rhythm; meters and rhythmic patterns; musical terms; seventh and ninth chords; and a brief study of a contemporary composition. No textbook is used, but handout materials and practice lesson sheets are used continuously.

Program Problems

Certain adjustments just be made for instrumental instruction because of physical problems. Students with arthritic hands have difficulty reaching certain chords on the guitar, especially those where the fingers are separated and well over on the fingerboard, such as the sixth string. Easier versions of chords are practical for these students. We also use guitar straps, because the students become quickly fatigued from maintaining the weight of the guitar in the correct position.

Dulcimers have a tendency to slide on the laps of students. Straps also prevent this and keep the dulcimer in the correct position. Another problem encountered in teaching beginning dulcimer is the student's tendency to play only the noting string and to omit the other two or three strings and drones. Difficult noting changes should be circled in pencil and studied before the pieces are played.

Autoharp students learn to play the instrument in many ways, including folk and scratch styles. The use of finger picks and varied accompaniments are taught, as well as the use of many types of strums. Initially, a chord chart is made, below the title of each piece, for all chords to be used, and these are practiced. Creativity in strumming and types of accompaniments is encouraged.

The recorder is more difficult for some students, particularly those with arthritic fingers. Also, the required memorization of fingering is difficult for certain students.

Music stands are absolutely essential for instrumental classes and orchestras. They can be moved close to students and adjusted. Also, in chorus, a set of music for each member is essential as vision problems are often involved.

Health problems also are involved. Health is always an important factor to consider. Many senior adults seem to be well and suddenly may be hospitalized for something that is quite serious.

Physical problems, involving the classroom and stage used for performance, include the necessity for shining the greatest amount of light directly over students, heat levels higher than those normally required, and air conditioning in hot weather.

Hearing deficiencies also require consideration. On stages that do not have good acoustical systems, a microphone should be used for the instructor where large groups are involved.

The area music program is free to all students. Many senior adults are on fixed incomes and it is essential that no one be inadvertently excluded for financial reasons.

A Challenge to Music Educators

At the present time, the next step to take in music education is extension of service to senior adults. This presents a challenge to music educators, whether they are retired or currently employed at schools, colleges, and universities or as musicians. The need is great for programs implemented by music or extension departments of schools of higher

learning and for those conducted in nursing homes, senior centers and clubs, places of worship, and housing centers for senior adults.

Anyone interested in working in this field should contact local, county, or state branches of the Council on Aging. Institutions and high-rise apartment complexes housing senior adults also could be sources of employment. Departments of university extension and music education at colleges and universities may also provide possible part-time, if not full-time, employment in the field. We must extend music teaching to include people of all ages for a lifetime of enjoyment.

Selected Readings

Bay, Bill. *Fun with Strums.* Pacific, MO: Mel Bay Publications, 1974.

Bay, Mel. *Modern Guitar Method Book I.* Pacific, MO: Mel Bay Publications, 1980.

Beidler, Franz. *Fun with the Recorder.* Pacific, MO: Mel Bay Publications, 1980.

Fun with the Autoharp. Pacific, MO: Mel Bay Publications, 1971.

Hughes, Virgil, *Fun with the Dulcimer.* Pacific, MO: Mel Bay Publications, 1972.

Ritchie, Jean. *The Dulcimer Book.* New York: Oak Publications, 1974.

The Many Ways To Play the Autoharp Vol. I. Northbrook, IL: Oscar Schmidt International, 1966.

Charles Elliott discusses the irony of a country with a rich heritage that has been transformed into one in which musical spectatorship predominates. Singing is an old, honored, and rich American tradition that needs to be revived. He offers some ideas for promoting singing at several levels in the community.

Singing in America: Reviving a Tradition

by Charles A. Elliott

America was once a singing nation. Throughout much of our country's history, singing played an important role in our educational, social, religious, political, and community activities. In fact, throughout the life of our nation, our history has been celebrated in song. The very first book printed in the English colonies of North America was the "Bay Psalm Book." There is a body of song to document the expansion of our nation westward and our evolution as a society through the social upheaval of the 1960s. Group singing was the primary activity in public school music education in this country for more than a hundred years. America has developed, in a relatively short period of time, a rich body of song unique to our people.

Tragically, community singing has suffered a major decline in recent years, a decline that has been, I believe, detrimental to society in general and to public school music education in particular. Ironically, this decline has occurred during a time in which the quality of choral performance is at an all-time high, especially in the public schools.

The extent of this problem was brought to my attention several years ago when I read a local

Charles A. Elliott is a professor of music at the University of South Carolina, Columbia. This article originally appeared in the January 1990 Music Educators Journal.

newspaper account of that year's International Scout Jamboree being held in Canada. A reporter had asked the American scouts in attendance for their impressions of scouts from other countries. Their first response was that they were impressed by how much scouts from other countries sang: when those scouts gathered together, they sang—songs from and about their native lands. Apparently, our scouts chose not to sing. This should not be considered an indictment of American scouts. Indeed, this is a situation that permeates our entire society. As a nation, we no longer celebrate our cultural heritage in song. We are becoming a nation of nonsingers.

Musical Spectatorship

Why has a country with such a rich heritage and tradition in community singing come so perilously close to abandoning that tradition? Should this trend be of concern to the music education profession?

As is usually the case, there are no simple answers, and the problem does not have only a single cause. It has been pointed out that, because television, computers, synthesizers, and various music-playback systems are readily available, one doesn't have to sing anymore to enjoy music. Most Americans have become musical spectators, and mass participation in music, especially vocal music, has become a thing of the past.

It may be that recent technological developments have contributed to the decline in community and group singing in this country, especially in the public schools, but I seriously doubt it. I believe that we as public school music teachers must accept at least a share of the blame. I also believe that we as music educators should be quite concerned about the declining role that group singing has played in our society.

Historically, the music education profession has espoused the beliefs that music can contribute to the well-being of the community and that all members of our society should be able to participate in the musical life of their communities in one form or another. Indeed, our motto for many decades with respect to the public schools was "Music for every child and every child for music."

In the early part of this century, music educators believed that an important part of their mission in the public schools was to teach every child about his or her cultural heritage through the fostering of a "common body of song." These educators thought that there were certain songs that every American child should know in order to fully participate in the life of the community. Group singing was not confined to the music class; assembly singing was a popular activity, and all music teachers were expected to be skilled in conducting effective assembly sings. The emphasis placed on group singing by music educators extended beyond the classroom and resulted in the publication of various books of songs used in community singing; among these were *18 Songs for Community Singing*,[1] *55 Songs and Choruses for Community Singing*,[2] and *Twice 55 Community Songs: The Green Book*.[3]

Even a cursory review of the history of public school music in this century will show a trend toward a de-emphasis on singing in the last twenty-five years of so, particularly for those students not enrolled in performance-oriented vocal groups. Beginning in the mid-1960s, the goal of those who taught general music (i.e., classroom music at the elementary level and "music appreciation" at the secondary level) was to teach students to "appreciate" music through an understanding of its "structure." Methods books were rewritten, and we were inundated with curricula that reflected the new "comprehensive" approach to teaching music. It became common practice for teachers to select songs entirely for their value in teaching predetermined "concepts." Singing for the sheer joy of singing was not highly valued.

New Goals

Granted, it is important that students understand how music "works" and that they are equipped with the tools necessary to make value judgments about the music that surrounds them on a daily basis. We have, however, so precious little time for music instruction, particularly for the vast majority of students who are not enrolled in one of the traditional performing ensembles, that choices need to be made and priorities must be set. It seems to me that our priorities for those students enrolled in the nonperformance music classes should be to ensure that they (1) leave the public schools with a positive attitude about music and value it as a part of their daily lives; (2) are equipped with the skill to participate at some level in the musical life of their communities; and (3) have some familiarity with their cultural heritage. Those, I believe, are goals that can be accomplished through group singing.

The community song movement is not a new idea, but it is an idea whose time has come again. I believe that MENC should once again undertake the task of identifying those songs we believe all American schoolchildren should be able to sing. The list should include songs we consider to be representative of our history and cultural heritage and songs that would allow our people to participate musically in their various religious, social, and community activities.

As music educators, we should consider the musical life of the entire nation to be at least partially our responsibility. We should be concerned that we have raised a generation of young people who are unfamiliar with the rich song heritage that America has to offer. Our people have been musically silent for too long now, and that silence is becoming deafening.

Notes

1. E. Casterton et al., eds., *18 Songs for Community Singing* (Boston: C. C. Birchard and Co., 1913).

2. Peter W. Dykema et al., eds., *55 Songs and Choruses for Community Singing* (Boston: C. C. Birchard and Co., 1917).

3. Peter W. Dykema et al., eds., *Twice 55 Community Songs: The Green Book* (Boston: C. C. Birchard and Co., 1923).

1612–07–1.5M–3/92